# The Outlook for Arab Gulf Cooperation

Jeffrey Martini, Becca Wasser, Dalia Dassa Kaye, Daniel Egel, Cordaye Ogletree

For more information on this publication, visit www.rand.org/t/RR1429

Library of Congress Cataloging-in-Publication Data is available for this publication.
ISBN: 978-0-8330-9307-3

Published by the RAND Corporation, Santa Monica, Calif.

© Copyright 2016 RAND Corporation

**RAND**® is a registered trademark.

Cover image: Mideast Saudi Arabia GCC summit, 2015
(photo by Saudi Arabian Press Agency via AP).

# Preface

This report explores the factors that bind and divide the six Gulf Cooperation Council (GCC) states and considers the implications of GCC cohesion for the region over the next ten years. The extent of cooperation among the GCC states also directly impacts American national security given the U.S. interest in enhancing regional stability, protecting the free flow of energy, and confronting a variety of threats emanating from the Middle East.

This study should be of interest to policymakers and scholars of the GCC, a regional organization comprised of Bahrain, Kuwait, Oman, Qatar, Saudi Arabia, and the United Arab Emirates. For policymakers, the report provides a framework for understanding political, economic, and security dynamics within the GCC, an expectation of future developments, and policy recommendations for securing U.S. interests. For scholars of the Arab Gulf, the report addresses gaps in the literature as GCC cohesion is an underexplored dimension in regional analyses. We seek to move beyond the basic observation that the GCC is not a monolith to better understand what unites and divides its members. This study also tackles GCC cohesion from a variety of disciplinary perspectives, examining current and future political, economic, and security trends out to 2025.

Funding for this study was provided, in part, by donors and by the independent research and development provisions of RAND's contracts for the operation of its U.S. Department of Defense federally funded research and development centers.

The research was conducted within the RAND National Security Research Division (NSRD). NSRD conducts research and analysis on defense and national security topics for the U.S. and allied defense, foreign policy, homeland security, and intelligence communities and foundations and other nongovernmental organizations that support defense and national security analysis.

For more information on NSRD, see www.rand.org/nsrd/ or contact the director (contact information is provided on the web page).

# Contents

# Figures and Table

## Figures

## Table

# Summary

The cohesion of the Gulf Cooperation Council (GCC)—defined here as the ability of the six GCC member states to act together or in parallel—is a major determinant of the influence of these strategic partners. As the United States seeks to enhance regional stability, protect the flow of energy, and confront threats emanating from the Middle East, GCC cohesion stands as a variable that could either advance or undermine U.S. interests.

Adjusting to the highs and lows of GCC cohesion is nothing new for U.S. policymakers. What is new is the extent of GCC regional activism, including military interventions, as its leaders perceive a weakening U.S. commitment to the region. While we disagree with this perception given the significant and continuing U.S. political and military commitment to the Gulf region, the perception of U.S. abandonment is nonetheless animating policies among the GCC states and cannot be dismissed. Many GCC leaders interpret the U.S. withdrawal from Iraq in 2011, the announced "pivot" to Asia, the approach toward the Arab Spring, the nuclear agreement with Iran, and limited U.S. intervention in Syria as an American betrayal of their interests. This changing context raises the stakes of U.S.–GCC engagement.

The current U.S. approach for adapting to the variable nature of GCC cohesion seeks to pursue bilateral and multilateral exchanges in a way that maintains flexibility. Thus, the annual U.S.-GCC strategic dialogue and 2015 Camp David Summit with GCC leaders are interspersed with bilateral exchanges. In terms of concrete policy initiatives, these span multilateral endeavors, such as joint ballistic missile defense, as well as bilateral endeavors, such as individual free trade agreements (FTAs). This report supports the continuation of that approach while suggesting several areas where multilateralism could be usefully expanded. These include providing incentives to the GCC to avail themselves of the ability to purchase defense material as a bloc, exploring the possibility of providing U.S. training to the GCC's Peninsula Shield Force (PSF), and considering whether the U.S.–negotiated bilateral trade and investment frameworks can be scaled up into a multilateral investment treaty.

The relative cohesion of the six GCC states varies considerably based on underlying conditions and the policy choices made by the GCC states, regional states, and extra-regional powers. In periods of high cohesion, the GCC states—Bahrain, Kuwait, Oman, Qatar, Saudi Arabia, and the United Arab Emirates (UAE)—are aligned on the major issues of the day and cooperate to enhance their overall capabilities. In periods of low cohesion, the member states are prone to working at cross-purposes and infighting can manifest itself in open rifts.

Standing together in the face of Iraq's missile attacks during the 1990–91 Gulf War and rallying around the Al Khalifa monarchy during the 2011 uprising in Bahrain represent high-water marks in GCC cohesion. Cooperation during these periods fell short of "all for one, one for all" but demonstrated the GCC's commitment to collective security even when that commitment entailed risk and cost. Conversely, the GCC "cold war" of 2013 and early 2014—in which individual member states cultivated different clients in Egypt, Libya, and Syria, culminating in Bahrain, Saudi Arabia, and the UAE withdrawing their ambassadors from Qatar—represents a low point in GCC cohesion. In this episode, shared interests lost out to individual member states attempting to maximize their influence in a transition period.

We argue that the degree of GCC cohesion varies over time but that intra–GCC cooperation operates within a band that includes a defined floor and ceiling. The floor of GCC cohesion is bounded by the exercise of coercive diplomacy in which the strongest collective within the GCC pressures outliers to conform to their position. But while diplomatic strong-arming is a feature of GCC politics, the use of military force against a fellow member state is not. Also falling below the floor of GCC cohesion is the collapse of the body; the sad fate of other subregional blocs like the Arab Maghreb Union. On the other end of the continuum, the ceiling of GCC cohesion is represented by joint foreign policy positions, including coordinated military action against external and internal security threats. The granting of capital and labor mobility across the GCC and financial support to the less-prosperous GCC states out of monarchical solidarity and regional stability concerns also are within the bounds of GCC cohesion. However, a full political union, monetary union, or the creation of an enforcement mechanism for decisionmaking within the GCC remains beyond the ceiling of GCC cohesion.

Understanding the scope and limits of GCC cohesion is crucial for interpreting the significance of developments within the bloc. There is a tendency by some observers of the GCC to inflate the importance of developments that are within the norm and cyclical nature of GCC cohesion. A particular member state finding itself at odds with the majority view within the GCC, as both Doha and Muscat have recently, is an expected feature of Arab Gulf politics. The six states tend to fall out, get back together again, and pair off. And a state that, in one period, is an advocate for closer cooperation, as Oman was in the 1990s with respect to its advocacy for an expanded PSF, can become an opponent of integration in different periods, as Oman is today with respect to the proposed monetary union and political union. This feature of GCC politics suggests the need to be discerning in interpreting which developments actually represent a shift in intra–GCC dynamics versus those that are part of the overarching cyclical pattern, but we find the conditions needed to fundamentally restructure intra-GCC dynamics, either toward more unity or greater division, unlikely.

Our historical review reveals several major factors that have promoted GCC cohesion. The factors include the necessity of the six states to band together to face mutual security threats, a shared interest in protecting their monarchical political identity, and a desire to expand access to consumer markets and take advantage of economies of scale in manufacturing and services. These factors have led the GCC to embark on ambitious integration projects within the security, political, and economic realms. The most notable achievements in these three domains are the creation of the PSF in 1982 and agreement on a mutual defense pact in 2000, the protection of the region's monarchical system during the 2011 Arab Uprisings, and the Economic Agreements of 1981 and 2001 that reduced barriers to the movement of capital and labor within the GCC.

The main factors working against GCC cohesion are differing threat perceptions, fear of Saudi hegemony, sovereignty sensitivities, and the lack of diversification within Gulf economies. These factors have operated as constraints on the GCC's development, and are manifest in members' resistance to integrate key military systems, cede foreign affairs decisionmaking to an overarching body, or establish a currency union. These differences are also evident in members supporting opposing forces in regional conflicts and seeking bilateral agreements with extra-regional partners rather than committing to negotiate as a bloc on economic matters.

Looking out over the next decade to 2025, many of the same factors that bound and divided the GCC states during the first 35 years of its existence are likely to remain operative. Added to those will be the near certainty of a generational change in leadership given the advanced age of current leaders, a potential shift in the regional security order based on Iran's evolving role in it, and further pressures to adapt to changes in global markets that include potential shifts in demand for energy. We do not find, however, that these changing conditions are likely to break the pattern of GCC cohesion that has characterized the bloc since it was established in 1981. These developments will undoubtedly animate new areas of cooperation and tensions, but we find the conditions needed to break the floor or ceiling of GCC cohesion unlikely.

Despite our projection of relative continuity in GCC cohesion, we are watching several possible stresses on the bloc's unity. One is potential differences between GCC members over endgames to the Yemen and Syria conflicts. While the Yemen conflict has largely unified the GCC states in their response, as it persists relationships may fray, particularly if the Saudis and Emiratis differ on what constitutes success. The Syria conflict has already generated disagreements over which factions to back on the ground and those differences could grow sharper should the conflict reach a turning point—either in the form of an Assad victory or the emergence of a reinvigorated insurgency capable of toppling the regime. In addition to military conflicts, another potential stress is GCC reactions to Iranian sanctions relief. The GCC states have different tolerances for economic relations with Iran, and the issue could force states to choose between economic and political objectives.

On the positive side of the ledger, the ten-year outlook for GCC cohesion contains several potential drivers of closer unity. For example, an increase in the Islamic State in the Levant (ISIL) threat could increase intra–GCC cooperation, particularly in the areas of intelligence sharing, coordination between internal security forces, and perhaps even provide a further push for the development of a joint internal security force. Increased intra-regional trade and growing infrastructure development could also contribute to GCC economic development over the next decade, even if we find monetary unification unlikely.

As the U.S. government looks to engage the GCC, policymakers will need to understand that GCC cohesion varies and has an important impact on what Washington will be able to accomplish with these partners, either bilaterally or multilaterally. And while it is tempting for the United States to attempt to engineer greater GCC cohesion in support of American policy aims, the United States faces constraints in the degree to which it can influence the trajectory of the GCC, most critically on the issue of how individual member states view their neighbors. Any attempt by Washington to shape GCC cohesion is likely to backfire, so the U.S. effort should be focused on adjusting expectations to the changing circumstances, particularly in light of Gulf leaders' perceptions of U.S. disengagement from the region.

Based on the variable nature of GCC cohesion, this report recommends that the U.S. government continue its current approach of mixing bilateral and multilateral engagement with the GCC. While critics of that approach will point to its inconsistency, we find that the approach operates as a useful hedge and is the norm for U.S. engagement with other regional blocs. Multilateralism provides a mechanism for advancing GCC cohesion when it aligns with U.S. interests, such as in the context of the counter ISIL campaign in which the United

States seeks GCC cooperation to roll back the group in Iraq and Syria. On the other hand, bilateralism can be used when the GCC is divided, or tempted to overreach. Bilateralism may also be a preferred approach when the GCC is showing signs of banding together for the purpose of pressing the United States for commitments it is not prepared to make.

While we support the continuation of U.S. policies of simultaneously working at both the bilateral and multilateral level with GCC partners, we believe the expansion of multilateral cooperation in some areas would be constructive. We see several opportunities for multilateralism on security issues. Specifically, we recommend the U.S. government push the GCC states to avail themselves of their abilities to purchase weapons together so as to better coordinate acquisitions decisions and foster interoperability. In the same vein, we recommend that the United States continue to work with the GCC states on integrated ballistic missile defense. As for softer approaches to enhancing GCC security, Washington should advocate for security dialogues that could eventually be expanded to include Iran. However, the inclusion of Iran in these dialogues would have to come at the initiative of the Gulf states with the short-term goal to engage Iran in establishing mechanisms for de-escalation of conflict, not integration of the country into a new regional security order.

In economic affairs, this report recommends that the United States continue to expand its bilateral engagements with the GCC states, building from the successful bilateral FTAs in the mid-2000s with Bahrain and Oman, but also leave open the opportunity for multilateral engagement. These agreements will benefit the United States economically, and be a stabilizing force for the GCC by creating new economic opportunities and encouraging diversification. Additionally, we recommend supporting the creation of a regional development organization, which creates transparency and gives equal representation to all six states in determining intra–GCC aid and investment flows, as a means to support long-term GCC prosperity and stability.

In the words of one Emirati interviewed for this report, the United States should embrace a policy toward the GCC states of "unite and rule" rather than reverting to "divide and rule."[1] We agree, with the caveat that the United States needs to continue bilateral engagement when multilateralism proves a bridge too far. In addition, bilateral ties should be retained as a hedge for those instances when GCC unity challenges, rather than advances, U.S. interests.

---

[1]   Interview in the UAE, September 20, 2015.

# Acknowledgments

This report would not have been possible without the help of many. The authors would like to thank all of those who participated in the "backcasting" exercise on Gulf Cooperation Council futures hosted by RAND in June 2015. We would also like to thank our Kuwaiti and Emirati interlocutors who provided frank and insightful observations during the September 2015 fieldwork for this report. The authors also offer thanks to the internal and external reviewers of the report, Ambassador Charlie Ries, F. Gregory Gause, III, and Andrew Parasiliti. All three reviewers provided thoughtful comments that greatly improved the report, although the views expressed in the report and any remaining errors belong to the authors alone. Finally, we thank John Tuten who assisted us with all the administrative aspects of this project.

# CHAPTER ONE

# Introduction

This report examines what binds and divides the six Gulf Cooperation Council (GCC) states and how GCC cohesion may evolve in the next ten years. Understanding the degree of cooperation, as well as the fissures within the organization, has implications for regional stability and security cooperation with the United States. Specifically, the relative cohesion of the GCC will shape how its members engage with a host of U.S. foreign policy priorities, including the counter–Islamic State in the Levant (ISIL) campaign; Iran's role in the evolving regional security order; conflict mitigation in Iraq, Syria, Yemen, and Libya; and the United States' enduring interest in maintaining energy flows from the region. GCC cohesion also represents an important factor in these states' own prospects for stability, which casts a shadow over all the specific issues of GCC-U.S. concern.

Our objective is to help policymakers better understand and prepare for future trends in a region with high stakes for U.S. strategic interests. Policymakers should better understand how GCC unity may advance or undermine U.S. policy goals in the region. For analysts of the GCC, this report addresses an important gap in the literature.[1]

---

[1]  The English-language work that comes closest to addressing our research questions is the excellent report from Jane Kinninmont, *Future Trends in the Gulf*, Chatham House, The Royal Institute of International Affairs, February 19, 2015. What distinguishes our report is its focus on those future trends that affect GCC cohesion and the implications for U.S. policy. Within the Arabic-language literature, the closest analogues are Mu'atz Salama, ed., "Ittihād Duwwal al-Khalīj al-'Arabīya: Afāq al-Mustaqbal" ["The Union of Arab Gulf Countries: Future Horizons"], *Al-Siyāsa Al-Dawlīya Journal*, April 2014; and Muhamad al-Rumayhi, *Al-Khalīj 2025 [The Gulf 2025]*, Beirut, Lebanon: Dar al-Saqi, 2009. These con-

---

**Box 1.1. The History and Organizational Structure of the GCC**

Bahrain, Kuwait, Oman, Qatar, Saudi Arabia and the United Arab Emirates (UAE) established the Cooperation Council for the Arab States of the Gulf, more commonly referred to as the GCC, on May 25, 1981. The founding charter focused on economics, education, and culture, with the aim of achieving "coordination, integration, and inter-connection . . . to achieve unity between them." Political and security issues were not expressly mentioned in the charter, although subsequent meetings and communiqués reaffirmed these areas of cooperation within the body.

The GCC consists of a Supreme Council, Ministerial Council, and General Secretariat. The Supreme Council is composed of the rulers of the member states and serves as the highest decisionmaking authority within the GCC. The GCC Ministerial Council, consisting of the member states' foreign ministers, meets quarterly. Each member also has the option to call an extraordinary session of either council, so long as another GCC member seconds the call. Within these meetings, each member state holds a single vote. There is a strong preference for consensus, but decisions are taken by majority rule when necessary.

A secretary-general chairs the GCC, and the chairmanship rotates among the six states. The current secretary-general is Abdullatif bin Rashid Al-Zayani, the former chief of public security of Bahrain. He is supported by ten assistant secretary-generals with functional portfolios, ranging from economic to cultural affairs. The GCC Secretariat and general headquarters are based in Riyadh, Saudi Arabia.

---

SOURCE: The Cooperation Council for the Arab States of the Gulf, homepage, undated(a).

Much has been written about the Arab Gulf, particularly from a security perspective, but GCC cohesion is an underexplored dimension in regional analyses. This report seeks to move beyond the basic observation that the GCC is not a monolith to better understand what unites and divides its members. This report is also distinct in taking an interdisciplinary approach of examining the political, economic, and security dimensions of GCC cohesion. Furthermore, it extends the analysis beyond the present to consider future trends out to 2025. The study does this while remaining focused on a single driving question: How do underlying conditions (e.g., energy markets, security environment) and policy choices affect GCC cohesion?

We use the term *cohesion* to mean the ability of the six GCC member states to act together or in parallel. Conceptually, this type of cooperation is described in Keohane's formulation as occur-

---

tributions, while important, lack our same focus on GCC cohesion, and both publications are the output of workshops rather than structured research.

ring "when actors adjust their behavior to the actual or anticipated preferences of others through a process of policy coordination."[2] This could take such forms as joint decisions reached in GCC ministerial meetings, the creation of a new institution within the GCC like a monetary union, or the development of an enforcement mechanism for GCC decisions.

Although the report aims to consider future trends through 2025, it begins from the premise that there is no surefire method for forecasting the future, and even less so in a region as volatile as the Arab Gulf. Rather than being predictive, the report offers informed judgments of what conditions and policy choices could lead to a more- or less-cohesive GCC. The report relies on a three-pronged approach to make these judgments. First, a literature review examines what has bound and divided the GCC since its start 35 years ago. The literature review grounds the report's future analysis in historical trends, understanding that straight-line projections do not help the analyst anticipate change.

Second, we conducted interviews with leading Arab Gulf experts from different disciplinary backgrounds (e.g., political scientists, economists, regional experts, business leaders) to test assumptions and initial hypotheses, as well as to elicit their views on future trends. The most structured of these discussions was a "backcasting" exercise that RAND hosted on June 26, 2015, with 15 experts under the Chatham House rule.[3] One-on-one interviews with Arab Gulf specialists, including fieldwork in September 2015 in Kuwait and the UAE, supplemented this exercise.

In analyzing the GCC's potential futures, the authors also relied on the proposition that cooperation between its member states, whether informal or institutionalized, is more likely when it is perceived to generate improvement in the welfare, security, and durability of the regimes entering into it.

---

[2]  Robert Keohane, "Cooperation and International Regimes," in *Perspectives on World Politics*, Little and Smith, eds., Routledge, 2006, p. 81.

[3]  *Backcasting* is an approach that begins by positing end states in order to focus on drivers that would push the outcome toward one hypothetical future or another.

These different inputs—the literature review, expert interviews, and general theoretical propositions—were then used to identify key political, economic, and security drivers likely to affect the future cohesion of the GCC in the coming decade. When scenarios are posited in Chapter Three, they are done so only to illustrate how these factors may play out under different conditions.

The report concludes with a discussion of policy implications for the U.S. government. Chapter Four begins with a review of current U.S. policy and then moves to recommendations on how the United States can engage multilaterally with the GCC and bilaterally with individual GCC member states to advance shared interests.

# CHAPTER TWO

# GCC Cohesion in Historical Perspective

This chapter considers the security, political, and economic factors that have shaped GCC cohesion since the organization's inception in 1981. The overall picture that emerges is of an organization that possesses sufficient shared interests and identity to cooperate, but is also limited by sovereignty concerns and internal rivalries that have thus far prevented the emergence of a more-robust union.

Despite strong interests in cooperation, the GCC states often require a crisis to break through the barrier of sovereignty sensitivities. These crises, such as the 1990-91 Gulf War or the 2011 uprising in Bahrain, do lead to periods of strong GCC cohesion in which the six states close ranks to face external threats and protect their monarchical systems from internal opposition. But this cooperation is not sustained and the GCC's institutional development, while full of such high-profile projects as the creation of the Peninsula Shield Force (PSF) and a Common Market, often overstates the level of true integration. The pattern suggests that absent a shift in GCC leaders' priorities, upticks in cooperation will be reactive to shocks that threaten the states' security or political structures rather than the product of a sustained effort.

## The Security Dimension of GCC Cohesion

Security both binds and divides the GCC. There are security concerns that increase the unity of the GCC, just as there are security concerns that exacerbate fractures within it. Whether or not the net effect of security is positively or negatively associated with GCC cohesion depends on the severity of the threat environment. The general pattern is that security crises that rise to the level of threatening regime survival are a forcing function for the GCC to overcome the legacy of historic disputes, uneven military development, fears of Saudi hegemony, and differences in threat perceptions that operate on the other side of the ledger. Conversely, more benign threat environments tend to bring divisions to the fore, undermining steps toward greater unity at precisely the time when unity projects could be pursued given the receding of the crisis.

Although not formed as a mutual defense pact, security concerns were a major impetus of the GCC's establishment. The organization's founding charter stresses cooperation in the economic and cultural domains, but the 1979 Revolution in Iran and the breakout of the Iran-Iraq war were important factors in the decision of the six member states to create a formal mechanism for cooperation in 1981.[1] If security began as an understood but unspoken part of the GCC's *raison d'être*, it did not take long for security to become a central part of the organization's efforts. Only a year after its founding, the GCC began to lay the plans for the establishment of a joint military force that would become known as the PSF. In 2000, the states formally committed themselves to a defensive alliance insofar as, "The member states consider any attack against any one of its members to be an attack against all."[2] In the past three decades, the GCC has been largely defined by its responses to the various security threats it has faced: from post–Revolution Iran, the Iran-Iraq War, the 1990–1991 Gulf War, the 2003 Iraq War, the popular uprisings that shook the Arab World, including Bahrain in 2011, to the recent military campaigns against ISIL in Syria and Iraq, and against Houthi forces and Saleh loyalists in Yemen.

The six states comprising the GCC do not always share a common threat perception or agree on the precise contours of the policy

---

[1]   F. Gregory Gause III, *The International Relations of the Persian Gulf*, Cambridge, UK: Cambridge University Press, 2009, p. 72.

[2]   This language comes from Article Two of the GCC Joint Defense Agreement that was issued on December 31, 2000 and subsequently ratified by the member states. The Cooperation Council for the Arab States of the Gulf, "GCC Joint Defense Agreement," web page, December 2000.

response.[3] However, security threats have served as a type of glue that binds together the states during times of crisis. For example, it was the threat of contagion from Iran's revolution and the trajectory of the Iran-Iraq war that led the GCC to establish a joint PSF. Just as it was the Tanker War and Iraq's invasion of Kuwait that led to the harmonization of key security policies—the GCC states' decision to reflag their vessels during the first crisis and willingness to host U.S. forces to dislodge Iraqi forces in the second.[4] During any of the security crises that have buffeted the Arab Gulf, individual states could have defected from the collective. This did not occur. The GCC states absorbed Iraq's Scud missiles together in 1991 and, two decades later, unified their positions on the unrest that threatened the Al Khalifa monarchy in Bahrain.[5] Cooperation has fallen well short of "all for one, one for all," but the GCC has endured even when there have been real risks and costs to cooperation.

That is not to say that the GCC member states are in lock step in their prioritization of security threats or their preferred policy responses. On the different security threats posed by Iran—be it conventional, nuclear, or asymmetric—Muscat is an outlier in preferring engagement and dialogue with Tehran.[6] And on the threat posed to regional security by political Islam in general—and, in particular, the Muslim Brotherhood (MB)—Doha was much more open to the MB's project than its counterparts. But these differences should not obscure

---

[3]   F. Gregory Gause III, "Threats and Threat Perception in the Persian Gulf Region," *Middle East Policy*, Vol. 14, No. 2, Summer 2007; Lynn Davis et al., *Iran's Nuclear Future: Critical U.S. Policy Choices*, Santa Monica, Calif.: RAND Corporation, MG-1087-AF, 2011.

[4]   Michael Barnett and F. Gregory Gause III, "Caravans in Opposite Directions: Society, State, and the Development of Community in the Gulf Cooperation Council," in Emanuel Adler and Michael Barnett, 1st ed., *Security Communities*, Cambridge, UK: Cambridge University Press, 1998, pp. 161–197.

[5]   Iraq launched 50 Scud missiles at Saudi Arabia, Bahrain, and Qatar during the 1990-91 Gulf War. See Yoel Guzansky, "Defense Cooperation in the Arabian Gulf: The Peninsula Shield Force Put to the Test," *Middle Eastern Studies*, Vol. 50, No. 4, May 2014, p. 646.

[6]   Yoel Guzansky, "The Foreign Policy Tools of Small Powers: Strategic Hedging in the Persian Gulf," *Middle East Policy*, Vol. XXII, No. 1, 2015a; Dalia Dassa Kaye and Frederic Wehrey, "A Nuclear Iran: The Reactions of Neighbours," *Survival*, 2007.

the fact that the six GCC states have usually come together with a common purpose in times of true crisis. Western and Arab scholars alike acknowledge this point. For example, Guzansky observed that "the history of the GCC countries has demonstrated that, when threats against them grew, it proved easier to put their disputes behind them and put forth an image of unity."[7] In a similar vein, Ayman Ibrahim al-Dasuqi notes,

> When the level of the threat is high, it overcomes the GCC states' internal differences and the sensitivities of the smaller states on the issue of sovereignty. . . . And when the level of threat is low, the differences between them show and the sensitivity over sovereignty reemerges . . . [8]

In addition to security threats, the GCC states share a common security guarantor. Before the advent of the GCC as an organization, the maritime security of Saudi Arabia and the Gulf littoral was provided by the United Kingdom (UK). For a period after the UK's withdrawal from the Gulf in 1971, the United States hesitated to take up the role of security guarantor. But after the Iranian Revolution and the Tanker War, the vacuum left by the UK was eventually filled by the United States.[9] Today, it is the U.S. naval presence operating from Bahrain, land forces stationed primarily in Kuwait, access to key air bases in Qatar, Oman, and the UAE, and prepositioned equipment that enables the United States to ensure GCC security from external threats.[10] The GCC states do pursue security cooperation with other extra-regional partners (e.g., France, India, Russia) and are showing

---

[7]    Guzansky, 2014.

[8]    Ayman Ibrahim al-Dasuqi, "Mu'adalat al-Istiqrar fi al-Nizham al-Iqlimi al-Khaliji" ["The Stability Dilemma in the Gulf Regional Order"], *Al-Mustaqbal al-'Arabi Journal*, No. 434, April 2015, p. 79.

[9]    John Duke Anthony, "Strategic Dynamics of Iran-GCC Relations," in Jean-Francois Seznec and Mimi Kirk, eds., *Industrialization in the Gulf: A Socioeconomic Revolution*, Washington, D.C.: Routledge, 2010.

[10]    Kenneth Katzman, "Iran, Gulf Security, and U.S. Policy," *Congressional Research Service*, May 28, 2015.

an increased willingness to take their own initiative, as demonstrated by the Saudi-led coalition attempting to restore President Abd Rabbuh Mansur Hadi in Yemen. But even with a more-activist GCC, the United States remains foundational to the regional security order and the deterrent of first resort.[11]

The United States serving as the security guarantor of the Gulf can work for and against GCC cohesion. It strengthens cohesion via the introduction of similar equipment and doctrine into the GCC states' military development.[12] And in times of war—such as the current air campaign against ISIL—it brings the GCC states into a unified command structure. In addition, the United States has often pushed the GCC to improve interoperability. Washington has a long-standing effort to work with the six member states on the creation of an integrated missile defense system. Conversely, the U.S. role as security guarantor can work against GCC cohesion insofar as the member states often default to using the crutch of external support rather than building internal capabilities to provide for their own security, something that would require greater intra–GCC cooperation.[13]

While common security threats are, on balance, drivers of Gulf cohesion, other elements of the GCC's security environment act as obstacles to cohesion. Territorial disputes over land and water rights have plagued the Gulf since the creation of modern states, notably Bahrain and Qatar over the Hawar island, the UAE and Saudi Arabia over rights to territorial waters and the adjacent coastline, and a disagreement among tribes from Saudi Arabia, the UAE, and Oman over the Al Buraimi Oasis. These disputes test the cohesiveness of the GCC, albeit in the form of political tensions and diplomatic flare-ups as opposed to actual saber rattling.

---

[11]  Anthony Cordesman, *The Gulf Military Balance: Volume I: The Conventional and Asymmetric Dimensions*, Center for Strategic & International Studies, January 2014.

[12]  The GCC states still face considerable challenges to interoperability. But the common platforms sold to the six states, such as F-16s and Patriot Air Defense Systems, create a baseline that would not exist if the United States was not the traditional equipper of choice.

[13]  Kristian Ulrichsen, "Gulf Security: Changing Internal and External Dynamics," London School of Economics, May 2009.

---

**Box 2.1. An Illustration of Sovereignty Concerns**

An ongoing dispute between Saudi Arabia and Kuwait over oil production in the "Divided Zone" is one example of where sovereignty concerns are evident among GCC states. Kuwait and Saudi Arabia have clashed over the building of a refinery in this shared territory, the granting of production rights to foreign oil companies, and the accrediting of workers operating in the area. All of these are symptoms of underlying tension between the two countries over how to divide the natural resource wealth in this area, which lacks precise demarcation. In 2015, this led to a prolonged shutdown of two fields—al-Khafji and al-Wafra. A letter from the Kuwaiti oil minister to his Saudi counterpart that held Riyadh accountable for the losses incurred by the stoppage was leaked to the press, touching off a media tempest over the minister's tone. This episode is just one of many that occur within the GCC and illustrative of the tensions that can boil up among the countries. But the fact that this dispute never threatened the broader relationship between Saudi Arabia and Kuwait speaks to the overall strength of intra–GCC relations.

---

SOURCE: "Khitāb Musarrib li Wazīr al-Naft al-Kuwaitī qad Yufāqim al-Azma al-Naftīya maʻ al-Saʻudīya" ["A Leaked Message from the Kuwait Oil Minister Could Exacerbate the Oil Crisis with Saudi Arabia"], *Al-Khaleej al-Jadid*, July 29, 2015.

At the forefront of the obstacles to cohesion is the smaller GCC states' fear of Saudi hegemony. Simply put, Saudi Arabia is an outlier in the GCC based on the size of its territory, population, military might, and economy, as well as the soft power it derives from its role as the custodian of the two holiest sites in Islam. As such, Saudi Arabia expects to play a leadership role in the GCC as a whole and the PSF specifically. Befitting the Saudis' weight in the organization, the GCC secretariat is located in Riyadh, the PSF has traditionally been based at Hafr al-Batin and headed by a Saudi major general, and the Saudis are not shy at drawing attention to their country's influence, with some proclaiming that its recent initiatives have elevated it to "the capital of Arab decisionmaking."[14]

Not surprisingly, that sentiment can rub other GCC states the wrong way, spurring fears that Saudi Arabia has designs to relegate the other five to junior members of the club. These anxieties tend to be strongest when the external threat environment is most benign. For example, it was in the mid- and late 1990s when Saddam Hussein was

---

[14]   Khalid bin Nayef al-Habas, "al-Saʻudīya wa Masʼūlīyat al-Qiyāda al-Iqlīmīya" ["Saudi Arabia and the Responsibility of Regional Leadership"], *al-Hayat*, May 13, 2015.

effectively contained and the Islamic Republic of Iran had yet to come to the fore as a potential nuclear power that the Gulf littoral states fretted most over Saudi dominance within the GCC. This was visible in the deteriorating relations between Doha and Riyadh. Qatar's former emir, Sheikh Hamad bin Khalifa Al Thani, who came to power by deposing his father Sheikh Khalifa bin Hamad Al Thani in a bloodless coup in 1995, was convinced that the Saudis were trying to reinstall his father as emir. This was also a period in which the smaller GCC states pressed for increased U.S. military presence on their soil. For the GCC rulers, an American presence had two advantages; it deterred the potential reemergence of the traditional security threats posed by Iran and Iraq], and gave the smaller GCC states a kind of hedge against Saudi hegemony via their own separate security ties with the United States.

Conversely, sensitivities over sovereignty and fears of Saudi hegemony recede when threats reach a critical mass. In 2011, Manama did not resist but rather invited in a contingent comprised largely of Saudi and Emirati forces, the two most militarily capable states in the GCC.[15] This was a simple case of the imperative of regime survival trumping the Al Khalifa dynasty's concerns over sovereignty.[16] The fear of losing a monarchy to the Arab Spring was so strong that one analyst described it as "breaking the glass ceiling" of GCC security cooperation.[17] Similarly, ISIL's advance and the Yemeni Houthis' move to depose the Hadi government presented the GCC states with security threats that trumped intra–GCC divisions in the 2012–2014 period over the MB's role in regional politics. With ISIL seizing Mosul and President Hadi having to flee Yemen, the countries of Qatar, the UAE,

---

[15]   Rashed Ahmed Rashed Isma'il, "Siyāsāt Buldān Majlis al-Ta'āwun al-Khalījī tijāh Tadā'iyāt Azmat Rabi' al-Thawrāt al-'Arabīya (Bahrain Anmūdhjan)" ["The Policies of the Gulf Cooperation Council Towards the Crisis of the Arab Spring Revolutions (Bahrain as an Example)"], *The Arab Journal of Political Science*, Nos. 43 and 44, Summer and Fall 2014.

[16]   In addition, Bahrain has a unique relationship with Saudi Arabia. Separated only by a causeway, reliant upon its larger neighbor for support, and navigating the challenge of a Sunni monarchy governing a restive Shi'a majority, Manama tends to defer to Riyadh.

[17]   Robert Mason, "The Omani Pursuit of a Large Peninsula Shield Force: A Case Study of a Small State's Search for Security," *British Journal of Middle Eastern Studies*, Vol. 41, No. 4, 2014.

and Saudi Arabia—the main antagonists in the feud over the MB—set aside the issue to launch joint military operations against these threats. It is when these types of threats recede that we are most likely to see old border disputes reemerge and other signs of GCC division. As observed by Barnett and Gause in the 1990s, "The GCC's trajectory seems consistent with alliance formation—formed in response to specific security threats, enduring as those threats endure, and fraying as those threats recede."[18]

## The Political Dimension of GCC Cohesion

Like security, politics can either unify or divide the GCC depending on the specific issue and context. Among the political factors that impact GCC cohesion, a shared interest in maintaining monarchical rule is the most important driver of unity. The monarchic identity of all six states, five of which are Sunni monarchies,[19] engenders solidarity among ruling families that eclipses their differences on narrow issues. This shared political identity is further reinforced by similar governing strategies built on ruling and patronage networks rooted in familial and tribal loyalties, as well as the rentier oil economy that has allowed the states to offer its citizens security, services, and benefits without the demands of taxation. The imperative of delivering on this ruling bargain has led to greater GCC cohesion as the wealthier states feel invested enough in the arrangement to support its continued viability throughout the GCC. On the other side of the ledger, sovereignty concerns are the biggest obstacle to greater GCC cohesion, although differing tolerances for political Islam and engagement with Iran also operate as wedge issues within the group.[20]

---

[18]  Barnett and Gause, 1998.

[19]  Oman's Sultanate is an Ibadi institution, although the Ibadi imam has not always supported the sultan.

[20]  We use *sovereignty* to mean each country's desire to retain independence in its decisionmaking.

It is difficult to overstate the imperative of regime survival in motivating state behavior, and this is particularly true in the case of the GCC states. Simply put, regime survival comes to the fore for the GCC states because their long-term future as monarchies is far from assured. These states are the exception in what has otherwise been the regional and global trend away from monarchies as a regime type. Before a wave of decolonization in the 1950s and 1960s, the Middle East featured more than a dozen monarchies stretching from Rabat to Tehran. Seven of those monarchies have since fallen,[21] leaving the six GCC states, the Hashemite Kingdom of Jordan, and Morocco as the remaining royal redoubts. Globally, the trend line has been even more stark. Only three absolute monarchies remain outside of the Middle East, and those are in tiny Brunei, Swaziland, and Vatican City.

The member states' preoccupation with protecting their political identities has given rise to the description of the GCC as a "monarchies club."[22] The dynamic is demonstrated by the GCC's relationship with its immediate neighbors, Iraq and Yemen, compared with its relationship with the other two monarchies in the region, Jordan and Morocco. At the time of the organization's founding in 1981 and again after the removal of Saddam Hussein, Iraq was not invited to join the GCC. Yemen (and before that North Yemen), which, like Iraq, is a republic with a sizable Shi'a population,[23] has faced a similarly cool reception to its inquiries about joining. On the other side of the coin, the GCC's announcement of accession talks with Morocco and Jordan in 2011 clearly belies the notion that geographic proximity or economic development are the driving forces of GCC unity.[24] If they were, the inclusion of Morocco would make little sense in that it bears

---

[21] The seven are the Hashemite monarchy of Iraq, the Kingdom of Egypt, the short-lived constitutional monarchy in Tunisia, the Pahlavi dynasty in Iran, the Senussi monarchy in Libya, the Federation of South Arabia, and the Imamate of North Yemen.

[22] Pierre Razoux, "The New Club of Arab Monarchies," *The New York Times*, June 1, 2011.

[23] In this case, the Shi'a population being referenced is made up of Zaydis who are perceived as Shi'a by the Sunni rulers of the Arab Gulf states. They may not self-identify as such and are distinct from Twelvers, who constitute the most common of the Shi'a branches.

[24] "GCC Studies Jordan, Morocco Membership Bids," *Gulf News*, May 11, 2011.

scant resemblance to its GCC counterparts by these measures. What it and the Hashemite Kingdom do share with the GCC is a Sunni monarchical identity, and it was no coincidence that the GCC invitation for these states to join came amidst regional turmoil that appeared to threaten this system of governance.[25]

In addition to regime type, political loyalty has reinforced GCC cohesion. The basic ruling bargain operates at two levels. Within royal families and between royal families and other elites, power sharing and cooptation are used to maintain allegiance. Ultimate authority rests in the hands of the rulers, but wealth and positions of influence are distributed across ruling families as a hedge against palace coups. At the popular level, the absence of genuine political participation is compensated through a model of governance in which loyalty is effectively purchased through the distribution of rents.[26] Oil wealth has facilitated the ability of the Gulf states to provide welfare and social services to bind the loyalty of citizens to the state, rather than to tribal, sectarian, or ideological identification. This loyalty has been essential to the maintenance of the Gulf states' state-society relations given the unique tribal and demographic makeup of these states, with the UAE alone comprising seven Trucial States led by distinct tribes. Since the collapse of one regime—or succumbing to pressure to devolve power via a constitutional monarchy—would set a dangerous precedent for the others, the GCC states attempt to insulate themselves and their neighbors from calls for political reform. Saudi financial support to Bahrain and Oman, which effectively subsidizes these neighbors' welfare systems, is but one example of common governing strategies binding the individual states.[27]

---

[25]  Morocco and Jordan are often included as observers in GCC fora, but they have not joined the GCC as full members. At the GCC summit on December 9–10, 2015, the relationship between the two states and the GCC was described a "strategic partnership" in the final communiqué.

[26]  Hazem Beblawi, "The Rentier State in the Arab World," in Giacomo Luciani, ed., *The Arab State*, Berkeley: University of California Press, 1990.

[27]  Kristian Ulrichsen, "Domestic Implications of the Arab Uprisings in the Gulf," in Ana Echagüe, ed., *The Gulf States and the Arab Uprisings*, Madrid: FRIDE and the Gulf Research Center, 2013.

These drivers of cohesion are sufficient to enable joint action by the GCC, but are insufficient to motivate the member states to cede sovereignty by agreeing to an enforcement mechanism for decisions taken by the GCC Secretariat. The GCC has established a political affairs arm, but in practice joint action is limited to those issues where consensus among the member states exists. This often takes the form of symbolic and relatively cost-free gestures, such as closing ranks when a member state is criticized. So, for example, the GCC in March 2015 issued a formal letter of protest to the Swedish ambassador in Riyadh in response to the Foreign Minister's "offending" statements about Saudi Arabia.[28] And, in June 2015, GCC Secretary General Al-Zayani issued a letter of protest to the Iraqi *chargé d'affaires* in Riyadh, contesting the Iraqi Foreign Ministry's criticism of Bahrain's decision to imprison a major Shi'a opposition leader.[29]

More significantly, policy coordination can rise to the level of GCC foreign ministers announcing, either at regularly scheduled ministerial meetings or at times of crisis, joint positions including the endorsement of military action. The GCC's call for the international community to impose a no-fly zone in Libya during Muammar Qaddafi's attempts to crush the uprising against his regime is one such example. By weighing in—and, in this case, ahead of the Arab League—the GCC provided the United States and its NATO partners an important regional imprimatur for the eventual operation. However, the aftermath of that operation clearly demonstrated the limits of GCC foreign policy coordination. The civilian protect mission in Libya began with Qatar and the UAE contributing to the same objective, but the two countries reverted to working at cross-purposes, supporting rival camps in a bid to advance different ideological agendas, when the military phase of the operation was over.

---

[28] The Swedish Foreign Minister had criticized Saudi Arabia for its lack of political freedom and record on human rights.

[29] "Duwāl al-Khalīj Tada'ū al-'Iraq ila Waqf Tadakhulātihi bi Shu'ūn al-Bahrain" ["The Gulf Countries Call on Iraq to Cease its Interventions in the Affairs of Bahrain"], *Al-Arabi al-Jadid*, June 22, 2015.

Among factors that limit GCC cohesion, sovereignty concerns cast the longest shadow. Historically, the smaller Gulf states have shifted between acquiescing to Saudi Arabia as the natural leader of the Arab Gulf while cultivating relationships with external powers as a hedge against Saudi hegemony. The state within the GCC best known for this approach in the 1980s was Kuwait, which succeeded in playing off global and regional powers to increase its weight in regional affairs, often annoying Saudi Arabia in the process.[30] The GCC countries' protection of their independent decisionmaking has hindered the ability of the GCC to create, influence, and implement common political goals. As Neil Partrick observed in 2011, "The GCC remains a cooperative alliance of states whose agreements have not fundamentally compromised their sovereignty, nor were ever intended to."[31] And sovereignty concerns are all the more visceral because they take place in the backdrop of longstanding territorial and maritime disputes.

It is the smaller GCC states in particular that are most exercised over maintaining their decisionmaking freedom of maneuver. These sensitivities were on display in 2011 when the late Saudi King Abdullah bin Abdulaziz Al Saud used the GCC summit to advance a call for full political unity, which the late leader renewed in 2013 and is consistent with the aspiration contained in Article 4 of the GCC's charter. The responses from the UAE and Kuwait were noncommittal while Oman voiced opposition, bluntly suggesting that a move to create a full political union would lead to its withdrawal from the GCC.[32] The episode also revealed how uncoordinated the body can be in that the smaller GCC states were surprised by King Abdullah's call for a political union in 2011, suggesting Saudi Arabia did not consult its fellow GCC members prior to the summit.[33]

---

[30]  Interviews in Kuwait, September 13–14, 2015.

[31]  Neil Partrick, "The GCC: Gulf State Integration or Leadership Cooperation?" research paper, Kuwait Programme on Development, Governance, and Globalisation in the Gulf States, London School of Economics, November 2011.

[32]  "Uman Tarfud al-Itthad al-Khalījī wa Tulawwih bi al-Insihāb" ["Oman Rejects the Gulf Union and Intimates Withdrawing"], *Al-Bayan*, December 8, 2013.

[33]  Interview in the UAE, September 18, 2015.

Sensitive political issues, such as the role of political Islam in the region and the wisdom of engagement with Iran, have also created fissures among the GCC states.[34] Qatar's pro-Islamist tendencies under Sheikh Hamad put it at loggerheads with Saudi Arabia and the UAE in particular. Differing stances on political Islam have played out in the Gulf, where Saudi Arabia and the UAE have banned the MB while Qatar, until recently, hosted and provided support to senior MB leaders; in Egypt, where a military takeover financially backed by Riyadh and Abu Dhabi deposed the Doha-supported MB government; in Libya, where Qatar and the UAE have supported rival government factions; and in the Palestinian Territories where Qatar has provided financial and moral support for Hamas.

These differences came to a head in March 2014, when Saudi Arabia, the UAE, and Bahrain withdrew their ambassadors from Qatar in protest over the latter's foreign policy. The group of anti–MB monarchies accused Qatar of not committing to the principles of the GCC, interfering in the internal affairs of their fellow Gulf states, supporting organizations detrimental to their security, and backing "hostile media."[35] The episode marked the apex of intra–GCC tensions over Qatar's foreign policy orientation, a rift which has been mitigated by what is generally viewed as Doha's capitulation to its neighbors by its expelling of MB leadership and shutting down of al-Jazeera al-Mubasher.[36]

However, underscoring that Gulf politics are dynamic and issues often cut both ways, the resolution of the incident can also be read as an example of partial GCC unity and even a small step in the body's institutional development. Despite many shared interests within the GCC, Saudi Arabia and the UAE are traditional rivals based on a ter-

---

[34] Guido Steinberg, "Islamism in the Gulf," in Ana Echagüe, ed., *The Gulf States and the Arab Uprisings*, Madrid: FRIDE and the Gulf Research Center, 2013.

[35] The three GCC states that withdrew their ambassadors from Doha in March 2014 issued a letter explaining the reasons for that move. Full text of the letter is available at "Al-Mamlaka, wa al-Imārāt wa al-Bahrain Tashab Sufarā'iha min Qatar" [The Kingdom, the Emirates and Bahrain Withdraw their Ambassadors from Qatar], *Al-Riyadh*, March 5, 2014.

[36] Al-Jazeera al-Mubasher was the al-Jazeera station covering events in Egypt from a pro–MB perspective.

ritorial dispute and competition for power and leadership within the Gulf. Riyadh and Abu Dhabi's pique at Doha's foreign policy brought the pair together, first to punish Doha and later to reconcile with it under the Riyadh Agreement of November 2014.[37] So while the Saudi-Emirati alignment was driven by a shared desire to strong-arm Doha, it also showed recognition that collective action can be an effective strategy to achieve their objectives. And in these efforts, Saudi Arabia and the UAE used institutions as their hammer, calling out previous agreements they claimed Qatar violated to justify their rebuke of it. The parties to the dispute also relied on Kuwait as an intermediary,[38] demonstrating some capacity for dispute resolution within the body even if tensions between Qatar and the anti–MB bloc within the GCC continue to simmer.

In addition to the issue of political Islam, engagement with Iran operates as another wedge within the GCC. In this case, Oman is the main outlier, having long maintained friendly relations with Iran.[39] The Omani strategy is variously described as "strategic hedging," "omni-balancing," or more creatively "Omanibalancing," in which Oman triangulates between the United States, Iran, and Saudi Arabia in an effort to maximize its leverage and mitigate security threats.[40] GCC counterparts tolerate Oman's approach, although its perceived legiti-mation of Iran can cause consternation in specific cases. For example, Sultan Qaboos bin Said Al Said of Oman broke ranks in becoming the first head of state to visit Iran's Mahmoud Ahmadinejad after the latter's disputed presidential victory in 2009. Even more controversial,

---

[37] "Qimat ar-Riyādh Tunhī al-Khilāf al-Khalījī maʿ Qatar" ["The Riyadh Summit Ends the Gulf Dispute with Qatar"], *Al-Arabiya*, November 16, 2014.

[38] Interview in Kuwait, September 13, 2015.

[39] Less forward-thinking than Oman but still out ahead of its GCC counterparts, Qatar has also showed openness to engagement with Iran. For example, Doha frustrated its neighbors when it invited Iranian President Mahmoud Ahmadinejad to the 2008 GCC summit, which in turn led Saudi Arabia to lower its level of representation in protest.

[40] Marc J. O'Reilly, "Omanibalancing: Oman Confronts an Uncertain Future," *Middle East Journal*, Vol. 52, No. 1, Winter 1998; Yoel Guzansky, "Strategic Hedging by Non-Great Powers," in Aharon Klieman, ed., *Great Powers and Geopolitics: International Affairs in a Rebalancing World*, Springer, 2015b, pp. 231–252.

Muscat's hosting of secret nuclear talks between Iranian and U.S. officials in 2012 and 2013 was seen by many Gulf leaders as a betrayal when its intermediary role was ultimately revealed. Most recently, Oman stood alone among the GCC states in not joining the Saudi-led coalition engaged in military operations in Yemen.

Underscoring the obstacles to GCC unity, nuances in the states' respective tolerances for political participation can also be a source of friction within the GCC. In particular, Kuwait and Bahrain have a history of granting more political freedom than Saudi Arabia, which, according to Freedom House, is the least politically free of the six GCC states.[41] Whereas Kuwait and Bahrain have tolerated political blocs and associations akin to parties, adopted universal suffrage, and operated parliaments with some—albeit circumscribed—authority, Saudi Arabia has no national level elections, no elected body with more than a "consultative" remit, and is only now granting women the right to vote in its municipal elections. When conditions favor unity, this variation in political freedom is little more than an interesting footnote. But at times of tension, the monarchies most resistant to participatory politics can look to their neighbors' experiments with reform as a challenge to their own legitimacy.

## The Economic Dimension of GCC Cohesion

The objective of economic integration is codified both in the GCC Charter and the 1981 Unified Economic Agreement (UEA). The GCC Charter includes economic integration as one of the GCC's four objectives, specifying in Article Four the intent: "To formulate similar regu-

---

[41] From 2005 to 2014, Freedom House has ranked political rights and freedoms in Kuwait and Bahrain as 4 and 5, respectively, on a scale in which 1 is the most free and 7 is the least free. Conversely, Saudi Arabia has never received a score other than 7 during that same time frame. One important caveat, however, is that Bahrain's political rights score has varied significantly in that same period. So while it is true that Bahrain has had a higher tolerance for political freedom than Saudi Arabia, by how much depends on the specific year. Historical data available at Freedom House, "About Freedom in the World: An Annual Study of Political Rights and Civil Liberties," web page, undated.

lations in various fields including the following: economic and financial affairs; commerce, customs and communications; education and culture."[42] And the UEA reiterates this call

> for closer relations and stronger links; and, [desire] to develop, extend, and enhance [GCC] economic ties on solid foundations, in the best interest of their peoples and for the sake of working to coordinate and standardize their economic, financial and monetary policies, as well as their commercial and industrial legislation.[43]

Success against these goals can be measured by an examination of intra–GCC trade, investment, and labor flows. Intra–GCC trade's share in total GCC trade has more than doubled since the GCC's founding.[44] Today, with intra–GCC trade accounting for an estimated 19 percent of all nonpetroleum GCC trade,[45] trade integration within the GCC is just below that of the Association of Southeast Asian Nations, in which intraregional trade accounts for 23 percent of trade.[46] The GCC still lags substantially behind more-established trading blocs,

---

[42]  The Cooperation Council for the Arab States of the Gulf, "The Charter," web page, undated(b).

[43]  World Intellectual Property Organization, "The Unified Economic Agreement Between the Countries of the Gulf Cooperation Council," undated. Words in brackets are modified to fit into the context of the sentence.

[44]  Steffen Hertog, *GCC Economic Integration: Focus on Nitty-Gritty of Convergence Rather Than High Profile Projects*, Gulf Research Center, September 2014.

[45]  Authors' estimates are based on Comtrade data for 2014. The reported value of 19 percent reflects country-weighted estimates, where each country's intra–GCC share is given equal weight. The comparable trade-weighted estimates, which give significantly more value to Saudi Arabia and the UAE given their much larger trade volume (roughly three to 10 times larger than the other four GCC states), indicate that intra–GCC trade accounts for 11 percent of all trade. Note that 2014 data are not available for Saudi Arabia or Kuwaiti and 2012–2014 data are not available for the UAE—our estimate assumes that (1) UAE intraregional trade grew at the same pace as the rest of the GCC for 2012–2014, and (2) Kuwait and Saudi Arabian intraregional trade grew at the same pace as the rest of the GCC for 2013–2014.

[46]  World Bank, "Economic Integration in the Gulf Cooperation Council (GCC)," 2010.

such as the North American Free Trade Agreement (NAFTA) or the European Union (EU).[47]

However, as demonstrated in Figure 2.1, intra–GCC trade's share in total trade has grown unevenly throughout the GCC's history. Although there seems to be a gentle uptick from 2012 to 2014, only two countries—Bahrain and Kuwait—demonstrate consistent growth in their share of intra–GCC trade. Others have been consistently high (Oman) or consistently low (Saudi Arabia and the UAE). Qatar, with an intra–GCC trade share of less than 10 percent in 2014, is at a near-

**Figure 2.1**
**Evolution of Intra–GCC Trade**

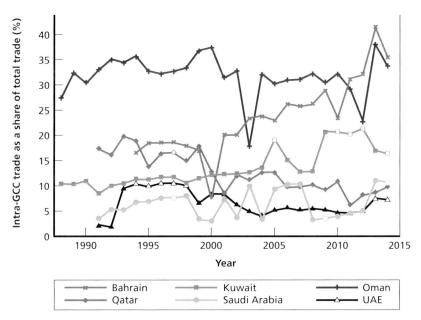

SOURCE: Data from Comtrade.
NOTE: Values reflect total trade (both imports and exports) with GCC partners as a share of total global trade. Missing data (indicated by hollow circles, squares, triangles, and diamonds) are interpolated based on annual changes in GCC share in other GCC nations.
RAND RR1429-2.1

---

[47] Intraregional trade accounts for 41 percent and 57 percent of all trade, respectively, within NAFTA and the EU-15 (World Bank, 2010).

historical low and significantly below the level of GCC integration experienced during the 1990s.

Intra–GCC foreign direct investment (FDI) has grown more dramatically. Intraregional FDI accounted for less than three percent of total FDI, on average, during the 1990–2003 period.[48] However, intraregional FDI surged to 16 percent during the 2003–2005 period,[49] with this dramatic increase attributed to the surge in oil prices beginning in 2003.[50] Intraregional FDI continued to grow, and accounted for 23 percent of total FDI during the 2009–2011 period.[51] Indeed, while total intra–GCC FDI flows accounted for only $3.6 billion from 1990 to 2003, intra–GCC investment during the 2000–2008 period has been estimated at nearly $30 billion.[52] Despite this surge in investment, it is important to note that intraregional FDI flows are concentrated in the oil sector and reportedly have done little to encourage technology transfer or increase export competitiveness.[53]

Moreover, the source of Gulf FDI is often governments rather than private-sector investors. A good example of this is the Gulf Investment Corporation (GIC), a GCC–operated institution in Kuwait that "has led or participated in initiatives with a total project value in the

---

[48]  Richard Shediac, Parag Khanna, Taufiq Rahim, and Hatem A. Samman, *Integrating, Not Integrated: A Scorecard of GCC Economic Integration*, Booz & Company Ideation Center, 2011.

[49]  United Nations Conference on Trade and Development (UNCTAD) Trade and Development Board: Investment, Enterprise and Development Commission, "Regional Integration and Foreign Direct Investment in Developing and Transition Economies, United Nations, December 3, 2012.

[50]  Shediac et al., 2011.

[51]  All growth in FDI between these two periods is attributed to the growth in intraregional FDI. Also, the GCC was the third highest in terms of FDI integration of the ten regional blocs reviewed by UNCTAD (UNCTAD Trade and Development Board: Investment, Enterprise and Development Commission, 2012).

[52]  Shediac et al., 2011.

[53]  Tim Callen, Reda Cherif, Fuad Hasanov, Amgad Hegazy, and Padamja Khandelwal, "Economic Diversification in the GCC: Past, Present, and Future," staff discussion notes, No. 14/12, International Monetary Fund, 2014.

tens of billions of dollars."[54] Essentially, the GIC operates as the venture capital arm of the GCC.[55] And while the GIC is in theory a force for private-sector development insofar as it invests in GCC–based companies with the aim of enabling them to expand operations or vertically integrate,[56] it is also an example of the GCC's government-driven approach to economic development in that it operates as a sovereign institution on behalf of the GCC states.

As for labor flows, the GCC countries are all significant labor importers given the small size of their domestic labor forces and GCC nationals' aversion to many of the jobs for which demand in the labor market outstrips supply, such as construction and the service sector. This gap is addressed through inflows of expatriate labor into the GCC countries and not by movement of labor across the GCC. In 2013, there were just 35,000 GCC nationals employed in GCC countries outside of their own.[57] Given a total of approximately 5.5 million GCC nationals in the labor forces, this means that only one-half of 1 percent of workers are availing themselves of the common market that allows for the free flow of labor within the GCC states.[58] And the low flow of labor is not serving as an engine of private-sector development, as roughly half of those 35,000 people are working in the public sector. It should be noted, however, that many wealthier citizens of the Arab Gulf are taking up second residences in places like Dubai, so they may

---

[54]  GIC, "Our History," web page, undated(b).

[55]  GIC maintained $2.3 billion in paid-up capital as of 2014. GIC, "GIC Financial Results 2014," web page, undated(a).

[56]  Interview in Kuwait, September 16, 2015.

[57]  "Qatar Ranks Third in Employment of GCC Nationals," *BQ Magazine*, December 9, 2014.

[58]  Baldwin-Edwards reports a labor force of nearly 5.5 million GCC nationals and more than 11 million foreigners as of 2008. Martin Baldwin-Edwards, "Labour Immigration and Labour Markets in the GCC Countries: National Patterns and Trends," Kuwait Programme on Development, Governance and Globalisation in the Gulf States, London: The London School of Economics and Political Science, No. 15, 2011.

also be doing business in these locales but are not counted toward the labor force.[59]

The nature of GCC economic integration shares a key limitation of cohesion with the security and political dimensions—namely, formal agreements overstate the level of real-world integration. The key difference: GCC economic integration has not been characterized by the same peaks and valleys experienced in the security and political dimensions. Rather, economic cooperation has been a fairly linear progression, albeit one that is still modest in the degree of integration achieved when judged against its lofty goals.

Economic integration is considered more palatable than security or political integration. Indeed, "from the outset the Gulf states had been more comfortable committing themselves to economic cooperation than to a security partnership."[60] At the time of the GCC's establishment, the member states were attempting to portray their cooperation as something other than a security alliance out of fear of antagonizing Iraq and Iran.[61] And within the sovereignty-sensitive GCC, economic cooperation was judged as more attainable than ceding decision-making over foreign affairs or merging their military capabilities into a truly integrated collective defense capability.

That said, it would be unfair to characterize the economic integration that occurred as a front for the GCC's real concern (i.e., security) or a lowest common denominator because political union is a bridge too far. Economic integration was perceived as a vital component of GCC cohesion, "necessary for continued political stability and prosperity in the Gulf."[62] These considerations help explain why the GCC has been able to avoid the same ups and downs that have characterized the political and security dimensions of GCC cohesion. For example, Saudi Arabia, the UAE, and Kuwait have long cooperated on maintaining oil prices within the Organization of the Petroleum Exporting

---

[59]   Interview in the UAE, September 20, 2015.

[60]   Partrick, 2011.

[61]   Barnett and Gause, 1998.

[62]   John Haldane, "GCC: Moving Towards Unity," *Washington Report on Middle East Affairs*, February 4, 1985.

---

**Box 2.2. An Example of a GCC Joint Venture**

Sohar, an aluminum smelter based in Oman, provides an illustrative example of a successful joint venture involving two Gulf states. It also illustrates that many of the business ventures in the Gulf are public-private partnerships, which affects the calculus that motivates these projects. The Sohar Aluminum Company (SAC) was founded in 2004 by the Oman Oil Company. Shortly after its founding, the Canadian firm Rio Tinto Alcan committed to a 20-percent stake in SAC. In 2005, the Abu Dhabi Electricity and Water Authority (ADEWA) committed to a 40-percent stake in SAC, leaving the Oman Oil Company with the remaining shares. In February 2005, the Oman Oil Company, ADEWA and Rio Tinto Alcan formalized their shareholders agreement to develop a $2.4 billion smelter in Sohar, Oman. Sheikh Diab bin Zayed Al-Nahyan, the chairman of ADEWA, noted that the project was a "landmark" in economic cooperation between Oman and the UAE. In 2010, ADEWA signed an agreement with the Abu Dhabi National Energy Company (Taqa) to transfer its stake in SAC to Taqa, thus shifting assets to its public company. Taqa's chief executive officer, Saif Al-Nuaimi, stated that this deal would "provide entry" for the company in Oman, highlighting Taqa's desire to do additional business in the country. As of 2015, the SAC smelter has an annual production capacity of 375,000 tons of aluminum.

---

Countries (OPEC). Within OPEC, the Gulf states have rallied behind often Saudi-led initiatives to set conditions within the international oil market.[63] Through OPEC, the GCC states have not only solidified their economic stability, but they also have used the forum as a platform to achieve political and security goals.

The second primary factor driving increased cohesion was the recognition that economic integration would enable access to larger markets and reduce transaction costs. This was a central component of the UEA, which "delineated ambitious goals for economic coordination aimed at eventual unification of economic, monetary, commercial and financial policies."[64] Economic liberalization within the GCC has received particular support from GCC technocrats who recognize the benefits from economic liberalization and integration.[65] The

---

[63]  Alex Lawler, "Saudi-Iran Rivalry Sets Scene for OPEC Showdown Over Output," Reuters, December 6, 2015.

[64]  Haldane, 1985.

[65]  Matteo Legrenzi, "Did the GCC Make a Difference? Institutional Realities and (Un)Intended Consequences," in Cilja Harders and Matteo Legrenzi, eds., *Beyond Regionalism?: Regional Cooperation, Regionalism and Regionalization in the Middle East*, London: Routledge, 2013. This article includes a discussion on the role of Gulf technocrats and civic orga-

result of both the UEA and continued support from technocrats and elites has been a suite of economic reforms, including the elimination of visa requirements for GCC citizens to move between countries, the relaxation of ownership rules for GCC nationals to operate enterprises across national borders, and the nascent common market and customs union established by the UEA.[66] In recent years, access to the GCC market has provided an important source of expansion opportunities for GCC–based private sector enterprises. These private sector enterprises have included both retail and production.[67]

However, several factors limit GCC integration. One commonly offered explanation for this low level of integration is a lack of diversification within the GCC economies. GCC countries are each heavily reliant on hydrocarbon exports. Only the UAE derives more than 35 percent of its gross domestic product (GDP) from sectors other than hydrocarbon export.[68] Without a diverse mix of manufacturing and service sectors, there are few opportunities for cross-border economic interaction not characterized by direct competition. The lack of complementarities limits opportunities for mutual economic growth and orients economic ties to partners outside of the Gulf.[69] But while analysts agree the Gulf needs diversification to drive sustainable economic growth, whether diversification would actually lead to deeper integration is uncertain. It may be that, for nonenergy-related manu-

---

nizations in the discourse of regional economic liberalization and integration. In addition, it asserts that technocrats view economic liberalization as a necessary precursor to political liberalization.

[66]  Legrenzi, 2013. To be clear, much of the UEA remains aspirational. As for the customs union, it was agreed to in 2003 but only fully implemented in 2015. At the time of this writing, there remain questions as to how fulsome it really is. A common market was agreed to in 1983, but barriers remain to implementation.

[67]  UAE-based Gulf Marketing Group's expansion into Kuwait and Saudi Arabia is an example in the retail sector (see Mary Sophia, "Sun & Sand Sports to Create 500 Jobs Across GCC in 2015," *Gulf Business*, February 2, 2015). An example from the production side is Saudi agriculture (see BMI Research, "Saudi Companies Well Positioned for Regional Expansion," web page, May 29, 2015).

[68]  World Bank, 2010.

[69]  World Bank, 2010.

factures, GCC countries are not competitive with the rest of the world, and GCC exporters will not be competitive in each other's markets no matter what economic reform is undertaken.

Second, intra–GCC competition in areas that "might otherwise offer scope for regional initiatives, such as finance, transport, and downstream energy" attenuate cohesion.[70] This propensity to compete against each other in these areas is illustrated by the recent moves of several GCC nations to seek preferential terms for trade or investment from abroad.[71] Because the GCC states have similar factors of production and are vying for similar markets, they compete against one another in areas including tourism, logistics, and aviation.

The internal competition is also illustrated by the World Bank's "Ease of Doing Business" index. Rather than moving together as a bloc to improve the business climate throughout the region, one GCC country—the UAE—has made considerable progress in improving its business climate, maintaining its overall place in international rankings, while the other five member states have regressed.[72] However, the similarity of the GCC economies can also offer a mechanism for increased integration, as has been demonstrated recently in the aviation sector. The GCC aviation sector, which accounted for 9 percent of total GDP and 13 percent of the nonhydrocarbon GDP in the GCC in

---

[70]  World Bank, 2010, p. 1.

[71]  Oman and Bahrain's recent establishment of independent bilateral free trade agreements (FTAs), rather than a single GCC–wide FTA, with the United States is illustrative. See Anja Zorob, "Oman Caught Between the GCC Customs Union and Bilateral Trade with the U.S.," in Steffen Wippel, eds., *Regionalizing Oman: Political, Economic and Social Dynamics*, June 2013, pp. 185–203.

[72]  The rankings for the six GCC countries are as follows: Bahrain No. 20 in 2010 and No. 65 in 2016; Kuwait No. 61 in 2010 and No. 101 in 2016; Oman No. 65 in 2010 and No. 70 in 2016; Qatar No. 39 in 2010 and No. 68 in 2016; Saudi Arabia No. 13 in 2010 and No. 82 in 2016; and the UAE No. 33 in 2010 and No. 31 in 2016. Data from Doing Business Group, "Doing Business 2010: Reforming Through Difficult Times," World Bank, Global Indicators Group, September 9, 2009; and Doing Business Group, "Doing Business 2016: Measuring Regulatory Quality and Efficiency," World Bank, Global Indicators Group, October 27, 2015.

2011,[73] has grown increasingly competitive with the recent emergence of three luxury airlines and several smaller airlines.[74] However, in 2015, when several major American airlines began lobbying the U.S. government to deny GCC airlines access to the U.S. market, the response of the Gulf airlines to these allegations was to fight them collectively.[75]

The third primary factor driving increased cohesion is the absence of adequate cross-border mass transit systems. Trucks, roadways, and shipping are the primary means for the movement of people and goods within the Gulf. The absence of other modes of travel, such as railways, has inhibited cross-border movement, ultimately limiting market expansion and growth.[76] This shortcoming is particularly notable given the GCC states' desire to position themselves as logistics and re-export hubs.

A fourth and final factor is the lack of harmonized financial statutes, regulation, and a weak financial services industry. In the absence

---

[73] Authors' estimates are based on (1) nominal total GDP of the GCC in 2011 at $1.45 trillion and (2) nominal nonhydrocarbon GDP at just under $1 trillion in 2011. See Air Transport Action Group, "Aviation Benefits Beyond Borders: Providing Employment, Trade Links, Tourism and Support for Sustainable Development Through Air Travel," March 2012; and Institute of International Finance, *GCC: Strong Diversified Growth, Limited Risks*, Washington, D.C., May 2014.

[74] Alpen Capital, "GCC Aviation Industry," March 3, 2014. Long-term growth in this sector is dependent on access to international tourist and travel passengers, including those based in the United States and Europe.

[75] The president of Qatar Airways is reported as saying that "Emirates and Etihad are my competitors but at the same time these are airlines of the GCC and it's the right of the GCC to respond to these unfounded allegations, lies against our carriers." (See Emirates 24/7 Business, "Qatar Airways Boss Slams U.S. Airlines on Subsidy Allegations," web page, July 10, 2015.) The argument is that these carriers are in violation of trade agreements stemming from the level of government subsidies received by Gulf airliners. Their case represents a major threat: If the United States or other large markets should restrict or deny landing rights to the Gulf airlines, the sector would contract. Moreover, similar public-private partnerships compose a significant portion of the GCC economy. If large swaths of the GCC export economy were to face countervailing duties and reduced access to international markets, the GCC would have to re-examine much of its current strategy for regional economic development.

[76] Frost & Sullivan, *Strategic Insight on the GCC Rail Sector*, October 21, 2011; World Bank, 2010.

of well-defined and fair rules governing the financial industry in the Gulf, financial institutions have struggled to expand their portfolios beyond domestic transactions.[77] Although capital flows within the region are growing, issues around the protection of foreign ownership rights discourage investment. To illustrate how closed off individual GCC countries are, only in 2015 did Qatar and Saudi Arabia grant licenses for the other's national bank to open branches in their countries.[78]

## Conclusion

The relative cohesion of the GCC is highly context dependent. In the security realm, the intensity of the threat environment and fears of Saudi hegemony are major factors that explain relations among the member states. In the political realm, a shared monarchical identity brings the GCC together, whereas sensitivities over sovereignty pull it apart. And in the economic realm, the benefits of economies of scale, access to larger markets, and lowered transaction costs along with some of the idiosyncrasies of Gulf business culture drive integration, while the countries' lack of a diversified economic base operates as a hurdle. In practice these factors have translated into halting progress toward building a more-cohesive GCC. But aspirations are well ahead of reality, and, compared with other regional blocs, the GCC lags in its level of integration.

---

[77] Eckart Woertz, *Financial Aspects of GCC Unification Efforts*, Gulf Research Center, August 2014. According to Woertz,

> Financing needs [in the region] have been met by an underdeveloped financial sector with only nascent regulatory institutions. The GCC financial sector is characterized by a lack of bond and derivate markets, difficult access to credit for small and middle enterprises, dominance of international banks in the project finance market, and heavily concentrated equity markets in terms of sectors and ownership.

[78] Abdullah bin Rabian, "Al-Mamlaka Akbar min al-Riyadh wa al Jidda Ya Sama!" [Oh Saudi Arabian Monetary Agency: The Kingdom is Bigger than Riyadh and Jidda!], *al-Hayat*, September 18, 2015.

# CHAPTER THREE

# Prospects for GCC Cohesion to 2025

As illustrated by the historical review in Chapter Two, the degree of GCC cohesion fluctuates based on numerous factors but stays within a defined band. There are chronic divisions among the states, but none portend a complete breakdown of the union or suggest that a member state will use force against another. On the other end of the spectrum, shared interests bind the GCC states but are insufficient to lead members to cede sovereignty to the GCC as a supranational institution. Absent fundamental changes in underlying conditions, this pattern is likely to continue over the next ten years. The specific issues that animate the GCC and align its members may shift over the coming decade, but the overall pattern, in which GCC cohesion fluctuates between its historical floor and ceiling, is likely to endure.

In order to help policymakers anticipate what intra–GCC dynamics may look like in 2025, this chapter begins by examining regional trends that we judge as likely to continue for that time frame. We then explore how these trends might impact GCC cohesion, concluding that these conditions will neither break through the floor nor the ceiling of the historical pattern of GCC cohesion. We then posit the less likely, but still possible, conditions that would alter the historical pattern of GCC cohesion. This approach serves the dual purpose of helping policymakers understand how new trends could play out within the bounds of the historical model and the outlier events that would break the pattern.

## Security: Projected Trend Lines

There appears to be a great deal of continuity in the threats facing GCC security in the next ten years compared with the threats the organization faced in the first 35 years of its existence. These include the threat from Iran (both conventional and asymmetrical), attacks from jihadi groups and lone wolves inspired by them, and the prospects of unrest from within. It is also reasonable to assume that the two fronts in the GCC's immediate periphery, represented by Yemen to the south and Iraq to the north, will continue to be a source of instability given that those countries have experienced protracted conflict for several decades now. In 2016, both countries are at a heightened boil.

Aside from a fundamental shift in Iran's orientation (discussed in the next section), the course of proxy conflicts that have spread throughout the region may have the greatest impact on GCC unity in the years to come. Although Syria, Iraq, Yemen, and Libya have strong domestic drivers to their conflicts, external involvement also plays a major role in sustaining the conflicts and shaping their outcomes. Because several GCC states are involved as direct belligerents or primary patrons of factions within these conflicts, how they evolve is likely to have a significant impact on unity. Of the three current conflicts mentioned, Yemen has engendered the most action insofar as all GCC states except Oman are participating in the military operation against the Houthis and Saleh loyalists. In the short term, that military campaign is providing a tremendous boost to GCC unity. Qatar and the UAE, only a year removed from supporting different factions in Egypt and Libya, are now fighting together to restore the Hadi government. And an outcome viewed as successful by the coalition participants will almost certainly provide a boost to Saudi leadership within the GCC and the Middle East.

Whether the Yemen campaign continues to promote GCC unity will hinge on the trajectory of the conflict. Over time, prolonged campaigns with high costs to participants tend to fray coalitions in light of different tolerance levels for sacrifice, and that logic would seem to apply to this case as well. While only the UAE and Saudi Arabia have suffered significant casualties to date, that situation could change should the coalition attempt to take and hold Sanaʻa. In addition to the open question of whether Sanaʻa changes the course and cost of the campaign, coalition participants will have to face two potentially contentious issues they have thus far deferred. The first is how to manage the southern secession issue among Hadi loyalists, many of whom favor a return to an independent South Yemen. And the second is the acceptability of al-Islah, Yemen's MB affiliate, in future governments. While the GCC has tabled earlier disputes over the MB, in this case it will be difficult to avoid the issue as al-Islah has historically operated as a key check on Houthi expansion. Differing tolerances within the coalition for MB participation already have emerged in the context of the appointment of an al-Islah representative as governor of Taiz after it was liberated from Houthi control.[1]

On the Syrian front, so long as President Bashar al-Assad and ISIL remain the strongest actors on the ground, the shared objectives of dislodging Assad, checking Iranian influence, and containing ISIL will tend to keep GCC members' strategies in sync. However, as the recent Libya experience demonstrates, it is in transition periods that GCC partners are most prone to competing for spheres of influence. Given the strategic weight of Syria as the one Arab state ally of Iran and an important actor in Lebanon, Iraq, and the Israeli-Palestinian sphere, the potential fall of the Assad regime could engender GCC rivalry over the future direction of that state. One could imagine, for instance, that the UAE would seek to support the most-secular forces on the ground given their strong ideological opposition to Islamists of all stripes. History would suggest Qatar would be more flexible in backing some Islamists in a post-Assad transition, while the Saudis would likely back factions taking the hardest line against Iran and Hezbollah. Looking at the Gulf experience in Libya, the competing visions of the GCC states were stark enough to be manifested in Qatar and the UAE militarily backing opposing sides in the post-Qaddafi order. The strategic stakes are even higher in Syria, which could either be a forcing function for better coordination or lead to a higher level of competition depending on the GCC states' respective risk thresholds.

---

[1]  Interview in the UAE, September 18, 2015.

With ISIL already having launched attacks in Kuwait and Saudi Arabia in 2015 and 2016, the current trend points toward an expansion of the Islamic State threat from Iraq and Syria into the Arabian Peninsula. ISIL may not have the wherewithal to take and hold territory in the GCC states, but it has shown the ability to carry out attacks inside these countries. The impact of this factor on GCC cohesion depends on the intensity of the threat and GCC policy responses, although there is good reason to believe the ISIL threat would help to strengthen GCC cohesion. ISIL threatens several of the common denominators that unite GCC members; namely, their investment in the state system, their commitment to monarchical forms of government, and their claims to religious and tribal legitimacy. Based on that and previous GCC responses to external threats, an increase in the ISIL threat should increase intra–GCC cooperation, particularly in the areas of intelligence sharing, coordination between internal security forces, and perhaps even provide a further push for the development of a joint internal security force.

Although the threat environment in the Arab Gulf is not likely to change significantly, there are shifts underway in the GCC's response to these threats. The most prominent development in this regard is the increasing activism of Saudi Arabia and the UAE. Riyadh and Abu Dhabi possess security forces that are capable by regional standards, but they have traditionally been reticent to employ these capabilities outside of Western-led international coalitions.[2] Recent developments suggest this may be changing. Whether judged by the Emiratis' decision to use air power against Islamist-aligned forces in Libya in 2014, or the leading role of the Emiratis in the ground campaign of the Yemen operation, the UAE appears to be growing more confident in its status as a regional military power.

As for Riyadh, it is noticeably more reluctant than Abu Dhabi to put forces on the ground in foreign conflicts, but it has not hesitated to use air power in Yemen (in 2009 and again in 2015) and has adopted a more-activist foreign policy in terms of speaking out on differences with the United States when their traditional security patron fails to

---

[2]    A notable exception is the 2009 Saudi use of air power against the Houthis.

meet Saudi expectations. In recent years, Saudi Arabia has voiced its displeasure through diplomatic walkouts, refusing to accept American outreach, ignoring U.S. recommendations to de-escalate confrontations with internal and external security threats, emphasizing cooperation with France over the United States, and exploring greater security cooperation with Russia.[3] This activism appears to have accelerated under the leadership of Saudi King Salman, but the trend predates him and thus may endure beyond his reign. After all, it was under the leadership of the late King Abdullah that Saudi Arabia turned down a rotating seat on the United Nations Security Council to protest inaction in Syria and gave a $3 billion grant to the Lebanese Armed Forces under the condition they buy French—and not U.S.—equipment.[4]

Nonetheless, neither the UAE's military activism nor Saudi Arabia's more independent foreign policy portends a shift in the pattern of GCC cohesion described in the historical review. These developments will undoubtedly figure in the relative unity of the GCC over the next ten years, but we do not anticipate them breaking the traditional floor or ceiling of GCC cooperation. At times, Saudi and Emirati activism may rally the GCC as it did when those two states marshaled the Gulf response to the 2011 uprising in Bahrain, when the pair strong-armed Doha to walk back its support for the MB in 2014, or when Saudi Arabia assembled a military coalition to confront the Houthis and Saleh loyalists in 2015. These are all examples in which the two strongest members of the GCC were successful in pulling the other

---

[3]  An example of a diplomatic walkout was then-Foreign Minister Saud al-Faisal leaving the "Friends of Syria" meeting in February 2012 in Tunisia in protest over U.S. inaction. In a similar vein, Saudi Arabia turned down a rotating seat on the UN Security Council in October 2013, reportedly for the same reason. An example of refusing outreach was King Salman bin Abdulaziz al Saud's decision to pass on attending the Camp David Summit called for by U.S. President Barack Obama to advance U.S.–Gulf cooperation. Among the security responses Saudi Arabia has pursued against U.S. recommendations was the military response to the Bahrain uprising and use of air power in Yemen even in the face of humanitarian concerns.

[4]  Saudi Arabia has since frozen aid to Lebanon in response to a perception that Beirut showed insufficient solidarity with Riyadh after its embassy was burned in Tehran in January 2016.

states along and the next ten years will supply future scenarios in which the same dynamics apply.

But on the other side of the ledger, Saudi and Emirati activism may lead to fraying, which also fits within the historical pattern of the GCC states falling out and coming back together again. For example, as the Yemen campaign drags on and casualties mount, it is easy to imagine unbalanced burdens within the Saudi-led coalition in Yemen leading to rifts between Saudi Arabia and the UAE on one level,[5] or between that pair and the smaller GCC states on another level. Similar disagreements could emerge over the strategic endgame in Yemen insofar as the five GCC capitals participating in the military campaign are unlikely to agree on the precise contours of what constitutes success and when the conflict is ripe for a negotiated solution. In the Levant, tensions could also emerge should Assad fall in Syria or retreat to a rump state on the Mediterranean. In that scenario, one could imagine different preferences emerging within the GCC on which factions to back and whether or not to send military advisers to support those factions on the ground.

Another projected trend line that will impact GCC cohesion, but without breaking the basic pattern, is GCC states moving to diversify their security relationships as hedges against perceived U.S. decline and weakening commitment. This process is underway and can be observed in GCC acquisitions decisions, such as the GCC states' purchase of French airframes and exploration of increased security cooperation with Russia—albeit with the latter seriously complicated by the foreign policy disagreement between Moscow and the Arab Gulf capitals on Syria policy. While some members of the GCC will continue to diversify their arms acquisitions and security cooperation as a hedge against the perception of U.S. retrenchment, we do not expect it to fundamentally change the cohesiveness of the GCC.

One reason security diversification is unlikely to disrupt the historical pattern of GCC cohesion is because its roots are already reflected

---

[5]  To be clear, Saudi-Emirati differences over Yemen have not yet publically come to the fore. Just the opposite, the UAE has been deferential to Saudi leadership even as it bears the largest burden in supplying ground forces.

in it. In the 1980s, Qatar and the UAE purchased Mirage fighters and flew these airframes in the 2011 Libya operation Unified Protector; today, these same states are purchasing Rafale fighters, while Kuwait is purchasing the Italian Eurofighter. Despite the Gulf states' desire to use France as a complement to the United States, Qatar, the UAE, and Saudi Arabia's air forces still largely consist of U.S. equipment that represents a sunk cost and ties the GCC states to an American operations and maintenance tail; in addition, all three countries have shown a strong interest in incorporating the latest American airframes (e.g., F-15, F-22, and F-35) into their forces.[6] A second reason this trend can be accommodated in the current pattern is that the six GCC states are not cultivating opposing patrons in a manner that would split the bloc into groups aligned with different extra-regional powers. And third, there is every reason to believe that the diversification is designed to increase the GCC states' leverage vis-à-vis the United States as its traditional security guarantor, rather than presaging a fundamental shift in the nature of the regional security order.

Finally, there are no indications that in the coming decade the GCC states will develop the PSF beyond a symbol of GCC commitment to mutual defense. Some of the GCC states are embracing military activism, but their means of projecting power are through their individual militaries rather than the development of a GCC–wide combined force. In three decades, the forces stationed at Hafr al-Batin have never deployed to a serious contingency; and, despite occasional reports of its development, there is no evidence to suggest the PSF is genuinely operational. Moreover, even in moments of relative GCC unity, such as the decision of four GCC states to join the Saudi-led military campaign against the Houthis in Yemen, the unanimity required to deploy a GCC–wide force rarely exists.

### Outlier Security Developments that Could Break the Pattern of GCC Cohesion

In 2015, the shared threat perception of Iran and the impetus it provides for most of the GCC states to cooperate in containing that threat

---

[6]   The United States has not agreed to sell the F-35 to any of the GCC states.

is one of the strongest unifying factors within the GCC. In a future scenario in which the Joint Comprehensive Plan of Action (JCPOA)[7] and shared interests in countering ISIL in Syria and Iraq lead to U.S.–Iranian rapprochement, the GCC states will face difficult choices. While our assessment is that a wider U.S.–Iranian rapprochement is unlikely, many in the GCC consider that outcome as the intent of U.S. policy.

Faced with broad U.S.–Iranian rapprochement, one choice would be for GCC states to join what could be perceived as an emerging new regional order by seeking to align themselves on issues where the U.S. and Iran are finding common ground, and to increase their own engagement with Iran in Gulf regional security dialogues. An alternative would be to actively resist a U.S.–Iranian rapprochement by pursuing foreign policies that are intentionally escalatory toward Iran to work against this outcome.

Based on past behavior, it would appear that a strategy of supporting Iran's inclusion as a partner in regional security would be more likely for smaller GCC states less committed to the Sunni-Shi'a and Arab-Persian dichotomies than Saudi Arabia. By this logic, Oman, Qatar, and perhaps Kuwait are all candidates for GCC countries as early joiners should a hypothetical U.S.–Iranian détente grow into rapprochement over the coming decade. Although these three states have their own bilateral concerns with Iran and share some of the threat perceptions of the other GCC members, they are more open to pursuing positive engagement with Iran than Saudi Arabia, Bahrain, and the UAE. Conversely, Saudi Arabia has a strong incentive to resist accommodation with Iran that would undercut its claim to regional leadership. And despite the potential for economic gain from trade and investment with Iran, the UAE generally shares the Saudi stance and adds to it the thorny issue of Iran's occupation of Abu Musa and Greater and Lesser Tunbs, the disputed islands claimed by both countries. As for Bahrain, its Shi'a majority population and proximity and

---

[7]   The JCPOA is the technical term for the agreement between world powers and Iran on the latter's nuclear program. It places limits on Iran's nuclear development in exchange for sanctions relief.

deference to Saudi Arabia suggests it also would likely be in the camp most resistant to such a shift in regional alignment.

A shift in U.S–Iranian relations for the better could divide the GCC according to the differing capabilities of the member states. The strongest members and those that seek the dominant position within the regional order, Riyadh and Abu Dhabi, are most resistant to integrating Iran into a regional order. Even if they were to take the leap of faith that cooperation with Iran would enhance their security, this realignment would shift them down a peg in the regional hierarchy, essentially reverting to the days of the "twin pillars" strategy when the United States banked on Saudi Arabia and Iran as the regional heavyweights. If Saudi Arabia and the UAE, as a rising power, do not want to share billing with Iran, they could be tempted to spoil the prospect by baiting the Islamic Republic into actions that make it unpalatable for the United States to consider integrating it into the regional order.[8] Should, for example, the Saudi-led coalition attempt to keep a large contingent of ground troops in Yemen, Gulf-supported factions in Syria focus their efforts on targeting Hezbollah fighters and Iranian Quds Force advisers, or the UAE attempt to confront Iran over the disputed islands, these actions would heighten tensions with Iran that would complicate the emergence of any U.S.–Iranian rapprochement. The approach also would work against GCC cohesion to say nothing of broader regional stability.

On the other hand, there is some possibility that a hypothetical U.S.–Iranian rapprochement would lead the GCC to move in parallel toward its own accommodations with Iran. That this remains a possibility is demonstrated by the warming that took place between Saudi Arabia and Iran when Mohammad Khatami was president of Iran in the 1990s.[9] The key difference, however, is that Iran of the 1990s, while still seen as a foe by the GCC, was less threatening to the GCC at

---

[8]   Dalia Dassa Kaye and Jeffrey Martini, *The Days After a Deal with Iran: Regional Responses to a Final Nuclear Agreement*, Santa Monica, Calif.: RAND Corporation, PE-122-RC, 2014.

[9]   Frederic Wehrey, Theodore W. Karasik, Alireza Nader, Jeremy J. Ghez, Lydia Hansell, and Robert A. Guffey, *Saudi-Iranian Relations Since the Fall of Saddam: Rivalry, Cooperation, and Implications for U.S. Policy*, Santa Monica, Calif.: RAND Corporation, MG-840-SRF, 2009.

that time than it appears to be today. In the 1990s, the GCC states could test improvements in its relations with Tehran without the prospect that the United States would get ahead of it in these efforts. Iran had yet to exert the dominant influence it now enjoys in Baghdad or develop a serious nuclear program, and Hezbollah, the Houthis, and other subnational groups aligned with Iran had yet to emerge as significant actors in what was still a state-dominated order. So while Gulf outreach to Iran in the 1990s ran the risk of legitimizing a "bad actor," it did not run the risk of legitimizing an ascendant regional power.

A related development to Iran's future role in the regional security order would be a Saudi decision to develop a nuclear program. Categorized here as an outlier development, Saudi Arabia's acquisition of nuclear weapons in the next ten years is possible but not likely.[10] However, the fact that former Saudi officials have openly called for the Kingdom to pursue a nuclear capability, and that current officials have refused to rule it out, suggests the contingency is plausible enough to merit treatment.[11] As it relates to this report, the key question is whether a Saudi bid to acquire turnkey nuclear infrastructure or develop it indigenously would lead the GCC to rally around the Kingdom or exacerbate schisms within the group.

In recent years, Saudi Arabia has been able to count on reflexive support from Bahrain, and given the latter's heavy economic dependence on its neighbor, this is likely to hold true over the coming decade absent fundamental political change in Manama. As for the other GCC member states, it is an open question whether they would support or oppose a Saudi push for nuclear weapons and would likely depend on the particular context. If Iran was found to be cheating on its commitments under the JCPOA or withdrew from the agreement based on its reading of Western noncompliance with the terms, this would logically strengthen the justification of the Saudis pursuing a

---

[10]    Colin H. Kahl, Melissa G. Dalton, and Matthew Irvine, *Atomic Kingdom: If Iran Builds the Bomb, Will Saudi Arabia Be Next?* Center for a New American Security, February 2013.

[11]    Alexandra Jaffe, "Saudi Ambassador to U.S. Won't Rule Out Building Nukes," CNN, March 27, 2015; Nawaf Obaid, "Actually, Saudi Arabia Could Get a Nuclear Weapon," CNN, June 19, 2015.

nuclear counter. But absent indications of Iranian deception under the JCPOA terms, neighbors could view a Saudi advance as unnecessarily escalatory and perhaps an opportunistic bid to advance its regional leadership. It would also constitute an awkward shift in Saudi policy because it and the other GCC states led a diplomatic push to establish a Weapons of Mass Destruction–Free Zone in the Gulf and Riyadh is a signatory to the Non Proliferation of Nuclear Weapons Treaty.

Additionally, the GCC countries that appear most exercised by the issue of Saudi hegemony—namely, Qatar, Oman, and Kuwait—would be candidates to resist being folded into a Saudi nuclear umbrella that would reduce them to adjuncts of Riyadh. Those states would also have concerns that an arms race would put them at risk of being collateral damage in a broader Saudi-Iranian military confrontation. The Obama administration has gone on record that a Saudi step in this direction would have fallout on the Kingdom's relationship with Washington,[12] and given Washington's enduring interest in nonproliferation, this sentiment is likely to extend to future U.S. administrations. So the smaller GCC states would be in the position of alienating a major security patron should they side with a hypothetical Saudi push to acquire. This all suggests that absent a heightened nuclear threat from Iran, Saudi pursuit of its own nuclear program would likely prove divisive within the GCC.

## Politics: Projected Trend Lines

Like security, the political outlook for the GCC in 2025 suggests developments unlikely to upend the historical pattern of GCC cohesion. A decade out we project that the region will still face rivalries exacerbated by enduring sovereignty concerns and splits over contentious issues, such as political Islam. While many of the political tensions within the GCC over the Muslim Brotherhood, Syria, and Iran are temporarily

---

[12]  President Obama's statement: "The [Saudis] covert—presumably—pursuit of a nuclear program would greatly strain the relationship they've got with the United States." See interview at Jeffrey Goldberg, "The Atlantic's Jeffrey Goldberg Interviews President Obama," *The Atlantic*, May 21, 2015.

muted today, the next decade will bring ample opportunity for these wedge issues to reappear and animate fault lines within the Gulf.

Foreign policy rivalries have long created fissures between the GCC states, albeit within the context of neighbors ultimately able to overcome differences when confronted by true crisis. In recent years, the role of political Islam, specifically support for the MB in the wake of the "Arab Spring," emerged as a wedge between the GCC states. The issue was largely settled in favor of the anti-MB camp, although reportedly Riyadh has begun outreach to the MB, which it previously outlawed as a terrorist organization, in an attempt to consolidate Sunni support against Iran and to avail itself of a potential partner in realizing its interests in Syria and Yemen.[13] Bahrain and Kuwait may also seek an eventual return to their norm of co-opting the MB. In Bahrain's case, the local MB affiliate played a role in maintaining the stability of the Al Khalifa monarchy in 2011. In Kuwait, MB members have been elected to parliament, although not as members of an official party. But from time to time the group has also called on its members to boycott parliamentary elections in Kuwait.

Given the historical pattern in which Islamist challengers are often subjected to waves of repression followed by rehabilitation, over the coming decade the UAE's position could shift from being the leader of a broadly-based Islamist roll-back to being isolated in its unbending opposition to the MB and other Islamist organizations.[14] It is difficult, for example, to imagine an endgame in Yemen that does not include using al-Islah—the local MB affiliate whose traditional base of support rings the Houthis' territory—as a check on the Houthis. In the same vein, outreach to the MB may eventually be considered as a way to promote stability in Egypt and further isolate ISIL elements in the Sinai. But if the anti-Islamist camp within the GCC moderates its stance toward Islamists over the next decade, it would fall within the historical pattern in which the GCC states and the broader region swings between an approach of uprooting and co-opting Islamists.

---

[13]  Yaroslav Trofimov, "Saudis Warm to Muslim Brotherhood, Seeking Sunni Unity on Yemen," *The Wall Street Journal*, April 2, 2015.

[14]  Interviews in the UAE, September 17 and 19, 2015.

Sovereignty sensitivities are also projected to continue between members of the GCC. This is due in part to the lack of effective dispute resolution mechanisms and in part that the GCC is an asymmetrical alliance insofar as Saudi Arabia is more powerful than its counterparts, although the UAE is closing the gap. Additionally, the push to include extra-regional countries, like Jordan and Morocco, could weaken the unity of original members who have differing levels of enthusiasm for GCC expansion.[15] If past experience holds, these sovereignty issues would operate as an upper bound on the level of cooperation the six states are willing to engage in, with sovereignty concerns being particularly salient during low threat environments while fading to the background during higher threat environments.

The Kuwaiti parliament's reservations over the GCC security agreement that allows for the extradition of wanted individuals between member countries is an example of how sovereignty concerns are likely to continue checking the institutional development of the GCC. In this case, Kuwait—the state with perhaps the highest level of political freedom within the GCC—is the site of considerable opposition to the agreement, largely driven by fears that it will be used to further "securitize" the region and erode civil liberties. A Kuwaiti political leader interviewed for this report, himself a descendent of the Najd region of Saudi Arabia, expressed concern that the Saudis would use the agreement to prosecute Kuwaiti citizens who may have transgressed Saudi but not Kuwaiti laws.[16]

Another issue that receives significant attention is the region's upcoming leadership change. In the report's ten-year outlook, several of the GCC states are likely to see succession after present leaders leave the scene. In particular, Oman, Kuwait, and Saudi Arabia are strong candidates given the age of their current leaders. And since at the time of this writing Kuwait's emir is 86 and the crown prince is 78, that country could easily face succession twice in the ten-year time frame of

---

[15]  Like the Kingdom's call for political union in 2011, it is suggested that Saudi Arabia conceived of GCC expansion without adequate consultation of its fellow members. Interview in the UAE, September 18, 2015.

[16]  Interview in Kuwait, September 14, 2015.

this report (see Table 3.1). In addition to the personalities, the modalities of succession may change if, for example, Sheikh Hamad's decision to abdicate and pass the Qatari leadership to his son Tamim is a harbinger of things to come in other member states. This course may also apply to Saudi Arabia, where the new monarch may have reason to firm up his succession line while he can still exercise influence during the transition period. While succession will inevitably open the door to change, there is no direct correlation between succession and GCC unity or disunity.[17]

Although all GCC countries except Oman have adopted succession practices that are intended to increase predictability in the transfer of power, these decisions are subject to change as demonstrated by Saudi King Salman's recent jettisoning of Crown Prince Muqrin in favor of Mohammed bin Nayef and elevation of his son Mohammed to deputy crown prince. But succession need not contribute to the inco-

**Table 3.1**
**Ages of GCC Heads of State**

| Country | Ruler and Age | Crown Prince and Age | Deputy Crown Prince and Age |
|---|---|---|---|
| Bahrain | HH King Hamad bin Isa Al Khalifa, 66 | Prince Salman, 46 | ___ |
| Kuwait | HH Sheikh Sabah al-Ahmad al-Jaber al-Sabah, 86 | Sheikh Nawaf al-Ahmad al-Jaber al-Sabah, 78 | ___ |
| Oman | Sultan Qaboos bin Said Al Said, 75 | ___ | ___ |
| Qatar | HH Sheikh Tamim, 35 | Sheikh Abdullah, 28 | ___ |
| Saudi Arabia | HH King Salman bin Abdulaziz Al Saud, 80 | Mohammed bin Nayef, 56 | Mohammed bin Salman, 30 |
| UAE | HH Sheikh Khalifa bin Zayed Al Nahyan, 68 | Mohammed bin Zayed, 55 | — |

NOTE: HH= His Highness.

---

[17] We determine this based on social science literature looking at alliance cohesion, which asserts that succession, except in extreme cases, rarely has a bearing on alliance survival. See, for example, Stephen M. Walt, "Why Alliances Endure or Collapse," *Survival: Global Politics and Strategy*, Vol. 39, No. 1, 1997, pp. 156–179.

herence of the GCC. Indeed, there are reasons to suggest a leadership change could be unifying under the right conditions. Sheikh Tamim's accession in Qatar, for example, provided the opportunity for Doha to turn the page on its souring relations with Riyadh. This could be part of an emerging trend in which younger Gulf leaders attempt to consolidate control in the early years of their rule by courting neighbors—and, in particular, Saudi support—to remove one threat in the initial transition period.

What will make this period of succession in the Gulf unique is the age of the designated successors. When Oman is removed from the equation because it has no designated successor and Kuwait is removed as the outlier in terms of the advanced age of its crown prince, the crown princes of the remaining four GCC states average just 46 years of age, more than 20 years younger than the current rulers. Youth should not be conflated with change as young rulers have strong incentives to be risk averse in the early years when they are still consolidating their rule. That said, the Gulf leaders of 2025 will bring a different outlook than the Gulf leaders of 2015. Some will have been born after 1971, a pivotal year in the Gulf when the UK withdrew from the region. Some, such as Deputy Crown Prince Mohammed bin Salman of Saudi Arabia, will have spent less time living in the West than his predecessors. And the successors are all but certain to be more wired and media savvy, and perhaps more in touch with citizen demands, than their older predecessors.

Change engendered by succession may lead to gradual political reform either instituted from above by new leaders or demanded from below. Kuwait is a state that could see increased political freedom and citizen participation in politics within the time frame of this report. While the line of succession in Kuwait is clear—78-year-old Sheikh Nawaf is the crown prince—the change in leadership may be an opportunity for modifications in Kuwait's political structure. As one of the more politically free countries in the Gulf, leadership change may provide an opening for even greater political participation, as it did during the 2006 succession when the Kuwaiti Parliament was able to extract concessions, including major electoral reforms, anticorruption measures, and media freedom.[18]

Bubbling below the surface are increased demands from Arab Gulf citizens for greater political participation and from foreign expatriate workers for equitable labor rights. Political disenfranchisement among Shi'a populations throughout the Gulf, particularly in Bahrain, will remain a contentious issue for the foreseeable future. This dissatisfaction could become more pronounced if the social contract used by rulers to maintain support from their populations through the provision of subsidized goods and services frays because of economic pressures. But as it relates to GCC cohesion, the threat of domestic uprisings has a unifying effect on the six states, who are invested in similar political systems and do not want to be exposed to the contagion of unrest in a neighboring country.

In addition to questions of foreign policy and political reform, identity politics will influence the prospects for GCC unity. Citizens of the GCC continue to balance multilevel identities that encompass nationality, religion, tribal affiliations, class, and geography. Some observe that a khaleeji identity, in which the people of the GCC states self-identify in regional (i.e., from *al-khaleej* or the Gulf) rather than national terms, is developing, which could provide a further boost to GCC institutional development. But there is no certainty that conditions on the ground will remain fertile for the continued growth of a khaleeji identity. For example, policy decisions, such as the introduction of compulsory military training for Emirati and Qatari males,[19] will have an impact on identity formation and may portend a dilution of khaleeji identity in favor of the national identity often engendered by military service.

Additional complicating factors in Gulf identity politics are the large sizes of expatriate communities and the variance of these popula-

---

[18]    Paul Salem, "Kuwait: Politics in a Participatory Emirate," Carnegie Papers, No. 3, Carnegie Endowment for International Peace, June 2007.

[19]    "UAE Introduces Compulsory Military Service," Al Jazeera, June 8, 2014; Nada Badawi, "Qatari Men Report for First Day of Mandatory National Service," *Doha News*, April 1, 2014.

tions within the GCC. The expatriate population ranges from a high of 89 percent in the UAE and Qatar to a low of around 30 percent in Saudi Arabia and Oman.[20] This demographic factor could slow the development of khaleeji identity as the GCC bifurcates into states where expatriates supplement a large national population base and those where nationals are increasingly scarce. For expatriate laborers, the existing kafala (i.e., sponsorship) system places them in a tenuous situation in which their employer essentially serves as the arbiter of workers' legal status. Reform efforts are underway but, unlike many Western countries, no GCC state has adopted a labor code that grants expatriate workers residence status, labor rights, or a path to citizenship.

While these developments—a potential return to the co-optation of Islamists, leadership changes, reform from within, and the evolution of a khaleeji identity—will help shape the Arab Gulf that emerges in 2025, none are sufficient to lead to a significant change in the basic pattern of GCC cohesion. They are interesting trends to watch, but can be accommodated within the historical pattern of a GCC that fluctuates between a loose alignment and a bloc capable of coordinated action.

### Outlier Political Developments that Could Break the Pattern of GCC Cohesion

Fundamentally shifting the pattern of GCC cohesion would require more extreme political change than we judge as likely in the time frame of this report. For example, while leadership transitions may not threaten GCC cohesion, full-blown succession crises could fray GCC unity in a scenario where states are tempted to meddle in a neighbor's succession process. As the royal families of the six GCC states have close relationships, a disputed succession process might provide the temptation for neighbors to back one aspirant to the throne or another. Although not likely, Saudi Arabia is a candidate within the GCC that could try to leverage its influence in neighbors' succession processes. Riyadh was accused of meddling in Doha's leadership dispute in the

---

[20] All numbers are from GCC Statistical Center, "Statistics," web page, undated. Qatar does not report its national versus non-national population, but estimates put it around the UAE's range of 89 percent expatriate based on nationals comprising 250,000 of a 2.22 million population.

1990s and there is a well-known schism within Bahrain's royal family between the crown prince and the conservative Khawalid faction that could invite outside interference.[21] And even if neighbors show restraint, should a claimant to the throne launch a palace coup, other GCC states may be put in the difficult position of choosing whether to legitimize the new ruler or fight to reconstitute the deposed ruler.[22] Any attempt by states to weigh in on their neighbors' succession processes is almost certain to erode GCC unity as all heads of state will come to fear a precedent that implies a loss of control over their dynasty.

In addition to succession meddling, a second outlier development that could challenge patterns of GCC cohesion would be the fall of a monarchy via a popular uprising. The likely effect would be a tug of war between contagion, on the one hand, and the remaining monarchies acting to reverse it on the other. While the 2011 deployment of the mainly Saudi-Emirati force in Bahrain suggests that the GCC states would be tempted to intervene militarily, they could also opt to inoculate themselves in the short term while sowing the seeds for a future reversal, akin to Egypt's experience between the January 25, 2011, and June 30, 2013, "revolutions." Either way, a breakdown in the monarchies club would most certainly erode cohesion by challenging the common political identity of the group.

A third outlier development that could shake up the historical pattern of GCC cohesion would be expansion of the GCC to encompass countries on the periphery of the current body, specifically Iraq or Yemen. Given the Gulf leadership's previous reactions to the desire of these nonmonarchies to join the GCC, this scenario should be viewed as remote. Perhaps the most likely path to it occurring would be if the Saudi-led military intervention in Yemen led to such strong ties with a future GCC–supported government in Sana'a that the Arab Gulf states became inclined to consider Yemen's inclusion as a sign of solidarity and a mechanism for tethering Yemen to the GCC.

---

[21]   Justin Gengler, "Royal Factionalism, the Khawalid, and the Securitization of 'the Shi'a Problem' in Bahrain," *Journal of Arabian Studies: Arabia, the Gulf, and the Red Sea*, Vol. 1, No. 3, 2013.

[22]   Interview in the UAE, September 17, 2015.

The potential impact of such a development on GCC cohesion, and why this scenario should be viewed as an outlier, is that it would be seen as a challenge to the GCC's political identity as a monarchies club, in addition to further straining the more-prosperous GCC states that already bear the burden of providing economic assistance to member states Bahrain and Oman. Finally, it would further introduce a challenging sectarian component given the size of Yemen's Zaydi population, although to be fair, Bahrain and Oman pose similar challenges in that regard. One could imagine that a move toward GCC membership for Yemen could create schisms in the GCC over questions of identity and economic burden. While the European experience demonstrates that it is possible for regional organizations to navigate these issues as the EU did when it expanded to incorporate less-prosperous Southern and Eastern Europe, identity has proven a bridge too far in overcoming reservations over Turkey's inclusion as a country with a distinct religious identity.

A final outlier development that would diverge from the historical pattern, albeit within the realm of the possible, would be Oman either withdrawing or being expelled from the GCC. Many interviewees flagged Oman as the "black sheep" of the GCC and not just for its different foreign policy stance on Iran.[23] Non-Omanis consider Oman culturally distinct from the remainder of the GCC and less invested in institutional development writ large,[24] not just as it pertains to the GCC. Added to that are perceptions that Oman is upset with the lack of follow-through on the economic assistance that was promised during the modest unrest in the Sultanate in 2011. Finally, there is a sense of betrayal among some Arab Gulf elites over Oman's positive relations with Tehran and lack of participation in the Saudi-led coalition in Yemen. This leaves Oman as the state with the most-tenuous relations within the GCC.

---

[23] Interviews in Kuwait, September 14–15, 2015; interviews in the UAE, September 17–19, 2015.

[24] One interviewee noted that Oman is not a signatory to many international treaties. Interviews in Kuwait, September 13, 2015.

## Economics: Projected Trend Lines

The next decade is anticipated to be a period of increased economic integration within the GCC, following the same gradual trend experienced from the 1980s through today. Deepening economic ties are anticipated to support GCC cohesion as member nations further explore joint economic enterprises, mutually advantageous economic policies, and new opportunities to enhance innovation and technical advancement in the region. However, the dramatic fall in oil prices during 2014–2015 threatens to overshadow other economic trends, as oil wealth has been relied on to fund many of these joint economic enterprises.

Two economic forces are anticipated to drive enhanced GCC integration over the next decade. The first is intra–GCC trade, which appears well placed to grow over the next decade. Intraregional trade quadrupled from 2003 to 2015 in U.S. dollar terms, and the recent establishment of a GCC customs union on January 1, 2015—even if it overstates the degree to which customs have really been harmonized among the states—should continue this trend.[25] The growth of the GCC's nonhydrocarbon sectors,[26] which have been supported by a vari-

---

[25] The Economist Intelligence Unit, "GCC Customs Union Up and Running," *The Economist*, January 13, 2015. Although several of the GCC nations have signed bilateral FTAs, these are unlikely to be divisive or "break" the GCC's common external tariff as has been suggested by previous authors (e.g., Zorob, 2013).

[26] GCC GDP growth in recent years has been dominated by growth in the nonhydrocarbon sectors. Kevin Körner and Oliver Masetti, *GCC in Times of Cheap Oil: An Opportunity for Economic Reform and Diversification*, Deutsche Bank Research, June 2015.

ety of regional and national strategies,[27] are also anticipated to deepen intraregional trade by increasing the breadth of tradable goods.[28]

Growing infrastructure development should also deepen GCC integration. GCC states have allocated tens of billions of dollars in regional transport and industrial infrastructure, including the development of a GCC power grid uniting the power transmission and distribution systems of the region.[29] A GCC Railway Network and new interstate highways, which are currently under construction and anticipated to cost nearly $100 billion from 2011 through 2020, could link all six GCC member states for the first time. GCC–wide efforts to develop infrastructure to reduce the risk of food insecurity are also underway.[30] However, the sheer scope of these regional infrastructure

---

[27]  In recognition that a lack of economic diversification restricts its economic progress writ large, the GCC has developed an ambitious strategy with the hopes of spurring the growth of the fledgling manufacturing sector. This strategy calls for "intensive investment in the non-oil manufacturing activities in order to reduce the dominance of a single source of income." The Cooperation Council for the Arab States of the Gulf Secretariat General, "The Revised Long-Term Comprehensive Development Strategy for the GCC States: 2010-2025," 2011. For a review of recent initiatives, see "Private Sector Innovation to Drive GCC Projects," *Arab News*, 2014.

[28]  Today, the manufacturing sector comprises 10 percent to 15 percent of GCC economic output. The preponderance of manufacturing activity is in energy-intensive products (e.g., petrochemicals, aluminum, construction materials, and plastics) with much of it concentrated in Saudi Arabia and the UAE. This sector tends to be either controlled or highly subsidized by GCC governments, which in lieu of protective tariffs, provide subsidized capital, water, energy, and infrastructure. This estimate is based on data collected and presented by Callen et al., 2014. State companies like Saudi Basics Industries Corporation, Aluminum Bahrain and Dubai Aluminum focus on heavy industry (see Steffen Hertog, "The Private Sector and Reform in the Gulf Cooperation Council," research paper, Kuwait Programme on Development, Governance, and Globalisation in the Gulf States, London School of Economics, July 2013). Private industrialists generally focus on products with low technology content and limited value added like cement, bulk petrochemicals, basic plastics, or agro-industrial products; see H.G. Mueller, "GCC Industrial Development," in G. Luciani, ed., *Resources Blessed: Diversification and the Gulf Development Model*, Berlin: Gerlach Press, 2012.

[29]  The power grid, which was completed in 2011 and cost $1.4 billion, is expected to save participating countries around $5 billion over its lifetime. Estimate from Frost & Sullivan, 2011; Shweta Jain, "Power Grid Brings GCC Economies Closer," *Gulf News*, April 25, 2011.

[30]  Food security is a perennial issue for the GCC as, due to the scarcity of arable land and water, the GCC imports some 80 percent of its food (see Rob Bailey, "Food Security Issue

projects pose questions as to their feasibility,[31] and failed infrastructure projects risk becoming symbols of mismanagement and waste.[32]

Although the overall trend line suggests a deepening of the GCC's economic integration, monetary unification, which has been a goal of the GCC since its founding,[33] still appears a bridge too far. As demonstrated by Oman and the UAE's recent rejection of the proposed monetary union, progress along this front is unlikely within a ten-year window given members' concerns about loss of control over monetary policy, to say nothing of the symbolic loss of sovereignty that comes with relinquishing national currencies.[34] And like the call for full political unity and for GCC expansion, non-Saudi members of the GCC tend to view the monetary union as an initiative thrust on them by Riyadh. For example, one Emirati interviewed for this report questioned why the Saudis brought the measure to a vote without consensus on an issue of such importance and sensitivity to all members.[35]

Other prominent economic sectors are anticipated to have a more-mixed impact on GCC integration, containing both unify-

---

for GCC is Linked to Supply, Not Prices," *The National*, November 11, 2013). One approach for reducing the risk of food insecurity, which is currently being developed, is the development of a GCC grain reserve (e.g., Joachim Braun and Maximo Torrero, *Implementing Physical and Virtual Food Reserves to Protect the Poor and Prevent Market Failure*, policy brief, No. 10, International Food Policy Research Institute, February 2009). Additional approaches to reduce food risk (e.g., pooled investment in food-related research) have also been proposed.

[31]  For the value of infrastructure projects either in the planning stages or underway numbers in the trillions of dollars, see Issac John, "GCC Expenditure on Track for $172 Billion Projects in 2015," *Khaleej Times*, June 1, 2015.

[32]  The railway will be a major test of the GCC's ability to work collaboratively. To date, the majority of progress on the railway network has been in Saudi Arabia and the UAE, while Qatar, Kuwait, and Bahrain lag behind. At the time of this writing, Oman has suspended work on the portion of its railway line that would link to the wider GCC network. A failure to create a truly integrated railway would cast a shadow over future joint development efforts.

[33]  Salem Nechi, "Assessing Economic and Financial Cooperation and Integration Among the GCC Countries," *Journal of Business & Policy Research*, Vol. 5, No. 1, July 2010.

[34]  A particular concern is that Saudi Arabia would not relinquish control of monetary policy to any of the other GCC nations, given Saudi Arabia's increased strength within the union.

[35]  Interview in the UAE, September 20, 2015.

ing and divisive elements. Education is an important example. The higher-education sector has boomed in recent years with the region now boasting some 65 public universities, 103 private universities, and 70 international universities.[36] This budding higher-education sector could help address some of the complex issues facing the GCC through applied research (e.g., labor, financial, and agriculture sectors), faculty and student exchange programs, and research corridors that support knowledge development. However, the education sector has become an arena for intra–GCC competition as GCC nations vie to establish partnerships with prestigious Western universities. Such competition may motivate prestige projects and substitute brand recognition for academic rigor.[37] Other sectors of the economy, including the development of the arts and cultural attractions, are experiencing a similar type of unproductive competition for prestige.

The fall in oil prices has resulted in the emergence of fiscal deficits for most of the GCC countries, with only Kuwait and Qatar running surpluses (see Figure 3.1).[38] Despite the accumulation of previous surpluses and the existence of sovereign wealth funds, a protracted period of low prices for oil will eventually constrain GCC spending.

In the short term, the GCC countries have sufficient reserves such that a reduction in spending will not be necessary. However, it is anticipated that the GCC nations will begin to reduce expenditures in the latter years of this report's ten-year outlook if oil prices do not rise significantly.[39] The consequences of reduced domestic spending

---

[36] This number is anticipated to continue rising over the next decade. See Julie Vardhan, "Internationalization and the Changing Paradigm of Higher Education in the GCC Countries," *Sage Open*, Vol. 5, No. 2, April 2015.

[37] Therefore, this may not incentivize the right outcomes for building the region's human capital because this approach has allowed the Gulf to shortcut the process of building out these institutions indigenously, but this also injects an element of competition over associations with top universities. This can take a positive form by encouraging a race for excellence. On the other hand, it can have negative effects as stated. See Vardhan, 2015.

[38] Bahrain, Oman, Saudi Arabia, and the UAE are all running deficits as the oil price has fallen below the fiscal break-even price of these GCC states.

[39] Martin Hvidt as quoted in Paul Cochrane, "GCC Starts Tightening its Belt on Glimmers of Future Austerity," *Middle East Eye*, April 21, 2015.

are difficult to predict, but possible outcomes could include a rise in domestic instability as targeted transfers are reduced. A second consequence would be the reduction of intra–GCC aid flows, which have been an important force for cohesion within the GCC. Since its founding, nearly $7 billion in aid has been provided from the GCC collectively to countries within the GCC, with the majority going to the two less-prosperous nations, Oman and Bahrain, who received 46 percent and 42 percent, respectively.[40] Less likely but possible responses to sustained low oil prices could include: (1) economic diversification, which could support deepening trade integration;[41] or (2) pro-market

**Figure 3.1**
**Fiscal Break-Even Prices Relative to Oil**

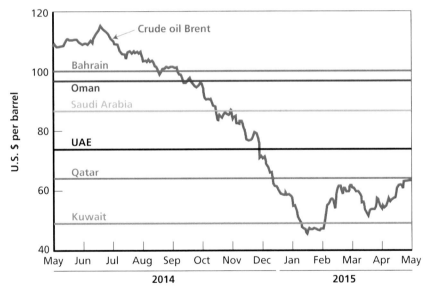

SOURCE: Asiya Investments, "Lower Oil Prices May Spur the Gulf to Diversify," 2015.
RAND RR1429-3.1

---

[40]   Authors' estimates based on AidData, "About Our Data Products," web page, undated.

[41]   See, for example, Körner and Masetti, 2015. Low oil prices in the mid- and late 1980s failed to induce diversification, but the recent rapid growth in the nonoil portions of the GCC economies suggests that conditions may be better now.

reforms, as demonstrated by the UAE's removal of gasoline subsidies in 2015 when prices were low,[42] which could encourage the development of the nonoil sectors of these economies.

A sustained period of low oil prices will not only affect the GCC's institutional development but also the pattern of GCC cooperation within OPEC. Today, the largest GCC oil producers—Saudi Arabia, the UAE, and Kuwait—are aligned in the long-term benefits of high production. The effort has an economic rationale in that it may drive out relatively costly production like that associated with the recovery of U.S. shale. The policy of high production also continues to put pressure on Iran, diminishing the economic relief Tehran will realize from the JCPOA. We do not believe this policy, as painful as it is for GCC producers in the short term, will lead to splits among these states. This is because the big three GCC oil producers are similar in that each has spare capacity and a relatively low fiscal break-even price for oil. While there are some differences in incentives and pain tolerances across the three, these states are in basic alignment on market fundamentals. Second, they share the same political motivation of checking Iran's power and low oil prices are in the service of that goal.

### Outlier Economic Developments that Could Break the Pattern of GCC Cohesion

Although the anticipated trend over the next decade is one of increased GCC economic integration, sanctions relief provided through the Iran nuclear agreement may create rifts within the GCC over individual member states' trade ties with Tehran. The removal of some trade and financial sanctions against Iran is likely to impact GCC cohesion via two mechanisms—oil prices and regional trade.[43]

---

[42]  Claudia Carpenter and Sarmad Khan, "UAE Removes Fuel Subsidy as Oil Drop Hurts Arab Economies," Bloomberg, July 21, 2015.

[43]  On present plans for implementation of the JCPOA by the United States, some sanctions will remain in place, giving the United States the ability to cut off a third-party country's access to the American financial system if these countries trade with Iranian entities designated on the Office of Foreign Assets Control list. Andrew Szubin, "Beyond The Vote: Implications for the Sanctions Regime on Iran," address to the Washington Institute, September 16, 2015.

As sanctions relief relates to oil prices, this development may reduce global oil prices by as much as $10 per barrel following Iran's "full return to the global market."[44] The lower oil prices resulting from new Iranian oil available in the global market could accelerate many of the financial pressures highlighted earlier.

As the nuclear deal relates to regional trade, GCC states' trade policies with Iran could emerge as a wedge issue if a subset of GCC states is tempted to put economics before politics in their relations with Tehran. The GCC and Iran became important trade partners during the late 1990s and 2000s, culminating in a planned GCC FTA in 2008 that ultimately failed because of the political climate.[45] By 2006, GCC exports to Iran accounted for nearly one-quarter of total Iranian imports. Although these GCC exports to Iran were dominated by re-exports passing through the UAE, Iran was also an important importer of nonoil exports originating in Saudi Arabia and the UAE.[46] However, GCC–Iran trade dropped precipitously under the sanctions regime against Iran, with GCC–Iran trade falling by nearly 50 percent from 2013 to 2014.[47]

---

[44] Estimated impact on global oil prices is from the World Bank (see World Bank, "Iran: Lifting of Sanctions Will Lower Oil Prices and Boost Domestic Economy if Managed Well," press release, Washington, D.C., August 10, 2015). Iran will require time to rehabilitate the deteriorating oil and gas infrastructure that currently holds back its production, though much of this work likely will be completed within a ten-year window.

[45] Will Fulton and Ariel Farrar-Wellman, "GCC-Iran Foreign Relations," Iran Tracker, July 21, 2011.

[46] See, for example, Nader Habibi, "The Impact of Sanctions on Iran-GCC Economic Relations," Middle East Brief, No. 45, Brandeis University Crown Center for Middle East Studies, November 2010; and Sumaya Ali, *GCC Economics: UAE-Iran's Trade Relations*, Securities and Investment Company, July 30, 2015. Note that the UAE was the largest exporter to Iran in 2014, accounting for $32.2 billion of a total of $96.4 billion in imports. Oman, Saudi Arabia, and Kuwait accounted for an additional $880 million, cumulatively. See International Monetary Fund, "Direction of Trade Statistics (DOTS)," web page, February 24, 2016.

[47] That dramatic reduction was disputed; see, for example, Hussein Ibish, *For Gulf Countries, Iran's Regional Behavior Overshadows Nuclear Deal*, The Arab Gulf States Institute in Washington, July 7, 2015.

The removal of economic sanctions against Iran could challenge some of the recent GCC unity exhibited in the foreign policy realm. In one scenario, differing tolerances for economic relations with Iran could lead to infighting between the GCC states, or in the case of the UAE, within a single federated state as Dubai and Abu Dhabi have historically had different approaches to trade with Iran. In the short term, the UAE and Oman are expected to be the greatest beneficiaries within the GCC of the removal of sanctions.[48] Given Muscat's positive relations with Tehran, it could be tempted to seek a preferential trade relationship with Iran as the latter emerges from sanctions. This would not only be contentious for its symbolic value, but would give Iran some access to the entire regional bloc as Omani re-exportation of Iranian goods should be anticipated given that Oman has consistently had the highest level of trade integration in the GCC. Oman has just barely been surpassed by Bahrain in the past few years, with some 30 percent to 40 percent of Omani trade occurring with other GCC nations (see Figure 2.1).

A second outlier scenario would be a break from the rentier model across the GCC. At present, there is insufficient pressure to motivate GCC leaders to undertake an initiative as politically fraught as reforming their social welfare systems. What reforms have being undertaken are largely superficial or designed to mute public outcry by focusing their implementation on politically weak constituencies. For example, the UAE's successful energy subsidy reform was largely absorbed by its expatriate population.[49] Attempts at deeper reform, such as Bahrain's removal of government subsidies on meat, were met with an outcry that led to the postponement and scaling back of the effort.[50] Given the political risks inherent in such endeavors, we judge it unlikely that

---

[48] For the UAE, see Karen Young, *Imagining Economic Opportunity in Iran*, The Arab Gulf States Institute in Washington, July 16, 2015. For Oman, see Ibish, 2015.

[49] Simeon Kerr and Pilita Clark, "UAE Drops Fuel Subsidies to Boost Finances and Cut Emissions," *Financial Times*, July 22, 2015.

[50] "Bahrain Postpones Plan to Remove Meat Subsidies," Reuters, September 2, 2015; "118,000 Families To Receive Meat Subsidy Payouts," Bahrain News Agency, October 2, 2015.

a GCC state will do away with rentierism in the ten-year time frame of this report. But extreme financial need or visionary leadership could lead to such a scenario and would challenge the reforming state's relations with its counterparts that continue to seek legitimacy based on the traditional terms.

## Conclusion

A ten-year time frame introduces considerable uncertainty into the prospects for GCC cohesion. Within that period the region will experience a generational change in leadership and could see major shifts in the regional security order or political transition. Notwithstanding these uncertainties, the GCC appears on track to remain within the historical pattern of GCC cohesion, which in the security and political dimensions is cyclical in nature, with periods of unity interspersed between periods of division. Breaking this historical pattern requires the introduction of outlier developments that are possible but unlikely. Absent fundamental shifts on the order of a U.S.–Iran rapprochement, the collapse of a monarchy, or serious intra–GCC splits over trade relations with Iran, the GCC of 2025 is projected to remain within the historical floor and ceiling of GCC cohesion.

# CHAPTER FOUR

# Policy Implications

Today and into the future, the Arab Gulf will be a major focus of U.S. policy. Among the most-pressing issues in the short term is reassuring GCC partners that Washington remains committed to the region's security, including checking Iranian support for terrorism and so-called proxy groups, despite some limited U.S.–Iranian cooperation. In the longer term, the United States would also benefit from encouraging GCC states to build a more-diversified and sustainable base for their prosperity and stability. As the U.S. government advances these efforts, the extent of GCC cohesion will help define the scope of what is possible in the realm of multilateral initiatives with the six states. And when U.S. outreach takes the form of bilateral engagement with individual member states, policymakers will need to understand the role of intra–GCC politics in reinforcing or constraining particular policy initiatives, and consider how the U.S. response to those requests will be interpreted in the six different capitals.

To be clear, the desire to better understand intra–GCC dynamics is not in service of an effort to game divisions between the countries. There are times when a cohesive GCC serves both U.S. and regional interests, and there are instances when GCC unity can challenge U.S. and regional interests. But the GCC's internal politics are its own to manage. For the United States, the goal is to understand when a cohesive GCC presents opportunities Washington should be ready to seize, and when unity or disunity presents potential challenges for which mitigating measures need to be readied.

## Current U.S. Policy

In the political and security realms, the U.S. government engages with the GCC in a variety of ways, at times reinforcing GCC cohesion and at other times following a hub-and-spoke model by pursuing individual arrangements with member states. In the economic realm, U.S. engagement primarily has been bilateral, although there is a gradual shift toward dealing with the GCC as a collective.

The multilateral approach in the political and security realms was evident in former U.S. Secretary of Defense Chuck Hagel's presentation at the December 2013 Manama Dialogue, when he said the United States should work with the GCC in "a coordinated way" and that a "multilateral approach [is] the best answer."[1] The subsequent U.S. decision to grant the GCC a NATO and African Union-like ability to purchase weapons systems as a bloc is an example of a U.S. policy that supports GCC cohesion (and, in fact, may have been ahead of GCC members' own vision for the institution).[2] Similarly, U.S. encouragement and support to the GCC to integrate their missile defense systems reinforces trends toward cohesion. President Obama's declaration of U.S. commitment to Gulf security from external threats was couched in regional and not bilateral terms, yet another example of U.S. policy endorsement for regional cooperation.[3] Finally, multilateral exercises also strengthen the interoperability of GCC militaries, albeit with the caveat that they often include non–GCC members in an effort to develop regional security architecture that is broader than just the GCC proper.[4]

---

[1]   Chuck Hagel, speech delivered at Manama Dialogue, Manama, Bahrain, December 7, 2013.

[2]   Awad Mustafa, "Hagel: U.S. to Sell Weapons to GCC States as a Block," Defense News, December 7, 2013.

[3]   The White House, "U.S.–Gulf Cooperation Council Camp David Joint Statement," Washington, D.C., May 14, 2015.

[4]   An example is the annual Eagle Resolve exercise, which involves the GCC states and takes place in the U.S. Central Command Area of Responsibility. U.S. Department of Defense, "Eagle Resolve Exercise Draws Worldwide Participation," March 20, 2015.

On the other side of the ledger, the United States engages in a variety of security cooperation that is bilateral in nature. Training with individual partners, such as that delivered to the Saudi Arabian National Guard, is more typical than engaging with joint forces like the PSF. And U.S. weapons sales to the region—while promoting interoperability to the degree that they come from the same source—are not necessarily designed to create complementary forces with particular areas of specialty, but rather to respond to the defense priorities of individual partners. The United States also avails itself of the differences within the GCC when that proves useful. In particular, the United States relies on Oman as a liaison to engage Iran or its allies like the Houthis even if that outreach, and Muscat's facilitation of it, can cause tensions within the GCC. Similarly, the United States is not wary of using the different countries' thresholds for hosting military forces or providing basing for combat operations to find workarounds for the reservations of other GCC states; although, to be fair, this approach is often welcomed by the GCC.

Politically, the United States tries to avoid becoming embroiled in intra–GCC disputes or political initiatives such as the call for full GCC

---

**Box 4.1. U.S.–GCC Defense Cooperation Efforts**

Both Democratic and Republican administrations have adopted signature initiatives aimed at advancing multilateral security cooperation with the GCC. The Bill Clinton administration instituted the Cooperative Defense Initiative, which sought to improve the interoperability of defense systems in the GCC. A subinitiative, Hizam al-Ta'wun (Belt of Cooperation), encouraged air defense information sharing, but was hampered by regional mistrust and sovereignty concerns.

In 2006, the George W. Bush administration established the Gulf Security Dialogue (GSD) as a mechanism to promote cooperation among the GCC member states and between the United States and the GCC over common threats. The GSD attempted to enhance regional military interoperability and build capacity in a variety of areas, including counterpiracy and infrastructure protection. Under the GSD, the United States encouraged the acquisition of missile defense systems.

The Obama administration has employed a variety of efforts to enhance regional defense cooperation. The U.S.–GCC Strategic Cooperation Forum was initiated in March 2012 to address Gulf political, security, and economic issues in a multilateral forum. This forum was supplemented by the U.S.–GCC Defense Ministerial, which focused solely on defense and security issues, in April 2014 in Riyadh. U.S. Secretary of Defense Hagel launched the Ministerial at the 2013 Manama Dialogue, where he also announced increased efforts to enhance a GCC missile defense framework and the sale of weapons systems to the GCC as a bloc.

union. That said, the United States can be drawn in inadvertently, as it was in 2012–2013 when the Obama administration's engagement with the Egyptian MB was seen as aligning with Qatar on a divisive issue within the GCC. Similarly, a push during the George W. Bush administration for integration of Iraq into the GCC raised contentious political identity questions, even though U.S. efforts to mend Iraq–GCC relations were based on regional security considerations and not a desire to challenge the GCC's common political identity or sectarian mix.

On the issue of Saudi influence within the GCC, the United States does its best to appear agnostic. At times, Washington defers to Riyadh's regional leadership position and, at other times, interacts with the smaller GCC states in a way that communicates a sense of equality in relations vis-à-vis Washington. An example of deference and out-ward respect for the outsized Saudi role in the GCC was affording Saudi Foreign Minister Adel Jubeir a meeting with President Obama right after the conclusion of the Vienna agreement with Iran.[5] On the other hand, the United States often works closely with Qatar and the UAE as two states within the GCC that have punched above their weight on foreign policy.

In managing economic ties with its GCC partners, the United States has typically followed a bilateral approach. This tendency was particularly pronounced during the George W. Bush administration, which negotiated a series of bilateral agreements with individual GCC nations rather than a single multilateral agreement. The United States signed FTAs with Bahrain (2004) and Oman (2006) and entered into six trade and investment framework agreements (TIFAs) with each GCC member state.[6] In a further nod to a hub-and-spoke model, the United States allowed several Gulf Sovereign Wealth Funds to pur-

[5]   The White House, "Readout of the President's Meeting with Saudi Foreign Minister Adel Al-Jubeir," press release, July 17, 2015.

[6]   The United States' bilateral approach irked Saudi Arabia and proponents of GCC unity, which saw the agreements as undermining the GCC's own economic integration project.

chase stakes in American manufacturers, financial institutions, and real estate on a bilateral basis.[7]

However, recent years have seen the emergence of a limited number of U.S.–GCC multilateral economic agreements. For example, the "Open Sky" agreement enables airlines from the GCC as a whole to operate relatively freely within the United States, although the policy is now under attack by U.S. flag airlines. The United States also recently entered into a 2012 Framework Agreement designed to increase economic relations between the United States and the GCC as a regional bloc, although the text of the Framework Agreement includes the clause that "in no way [does the agreement] affect the authority of the United States to undertake bilateral activities with individual GCC member states . . . or conclude bilateral agreements with individual GCC member states."[8]

## Policy Recommendations

GCC cohesion advances U.S. interests by enabling Washington to partner with a more capable collective pursuing common goals. GCC unity can contribute to its members' political stability, self-defense capabilities, and prospects for sustained economic growth; outcomes the United States supports and is invested in. However, there are instances when GCC unity can challenge U.S. interests, for example, when unity enables the GCC to take escalatory military action or crack down on political opposition under the pretext of internal security concerns. On balance, the authors see more opportunity than risk in GCC unity, and thus recommend a modest increase in multilateral initiatives while still retaining strong bilateral relationships as a hedge.

---

[7]   Nader Habibi and Eckart Woertz, "U.S.–Arab Economic Relations and the Obama Administration," Middle East Brief, No. 34, Brandeis University Crown Center for Middle East Studies, February 2009.

[8]   Office of the U.S. Trade Representative, "Framework Agreement for Trade, Economic, Investment and Technical Cooperation Between the Cooperation Council for the Arab States and the Government of the United States of America," 2012.

In terms of specific initiatives, the United States should more strongly incentivize its GCC partners to purchase weapons systems collectively, which would serve as a mechanism for GCC states to coordinate their acquisitions strategies and potentially evolve into more capable security partners. The United States might accomplish this through inducements, by putting systems on the table that Washington would sell to the GCC in a purchase negotiated collectively—but not if a single member state requests the system bilaterally. Sticks are unlikely to work because the United States also receives a benefit from arms sales to the Gulf—in the form of support to American defense industries and the building of more-capable partners—and, although the United States remains the equipper of choice, GCC states have alternative equippers, including Western powers (such as France or the UK) and their extra-regional competitors (such as Russia and China).

On training, the United States should consider providing training to the PSF to combat military and terrorist threats, rather than as an instrument to put down political unrest. The focus should be on professionalization. For example, the United States could consider training in nonlethal crowd dispersal that orients the force to operate in a less-repressive way if it is again called upon to execute what amounts to an internal security role. The State Department—in particular, its Bureau of International Narcotics and Law Enforcement—can also be a vehicle for providing training to internal security forces and judiciaries. As the GCC embarks on greater integration of these sectors based on the security agreement that has now been ratified by all GCC members except Kuwait, the collective will face challenges in harmonizing law enforcement and judicial practices toward which State Department programs could make a positive contribution.

Achieving a truly integrated joint ballistic missile defense system has been slow to materialize given sovereignty concerns. But Washington should continue pushing this initiative, because a joint ballistic missile defense system provides one of the greatest practical benefits of cooperation. The logic is based on warning time. GCC states would have but a few minutes to react to the potential launch of Iranian ballistic missiles before a decision would have to be taken to intercept. At present, several of the GCC states do not wish to cede that launch authority to a command and control center that would need to be based in a single location and act on the basis of protocols without the need for further intra–GCC deliberation.[9] Another obstacle is that the joint ballistic missile defense system would require the GCC to prioritize the territory it would defend from ballistic missile attack, creating an uncomfortable situation in which some states would have more of their territory covered as first-tier priorities. But the consequence of not moving ahead on joint ballistic missile defense is an erosion of GCC deterrence, so the United States is right to continue pressing the issue despite the obstacles it faces.

As has been an issue at least dating back to the end of the 1990-91 Gulf War, the U.S. government will also need to grapple with how it sees non–GCC states contributing to Gulf security. Several formulas have been tried, such as 6 + 2; originally, the six GCC states plus Syria and Egypt after Damascus sided with the coalition in expelling Saddam Hussein from Kuwait. More recently, the formula has been the six GCC states with Jordan and Egypt providing additional strategic depth and much-needed manpower to the GCC. This raises the question of how the United States prefers to see the two non–GCC members (Jordan and Egypt) formally or informally integrated into regional partnerships. The U.S. approach to the organization of Eagle Resolve, a joint exercise that for the first time in 2015 included all of the GCC states plus Egypt and Jordan—suggests Washington sees those eight Arab states as the backbone of the current regional security order. But whether that means the United States should endorse and push for formal integration of Jordan as a full GCC member remains an open question. And more formal integration of Egypt into regional security structures at a time when its military is exercising political control is a complicating factor.

Whatever the U.S. vision, linking GCC states to their strategic depth from the West would not seem to require new institutions. Egypt and Jordan possess robust security cooperation with their Arab Gulf neighbors, and Jordan, while not a full member of the GCC, effectively operates as an adjunct of the organization. The United States,

---

[9]   Interview in the UAE, September 17, 2015.

however, would do better to highlight the Jordanian military model to their GCC counterparts rather than the Egyptian model. Jordan's military has built a well-earned reputation as a professionalized force genuinely interested in training and capacity building, whereas Egypt's military, while capable in regional terms, has built a reputation for dependence on Foreign Military Financing and the development of its business interests in Egypt. This is certainly not a model the United States has a desire to see take hold among its Arab Gulf partners, so highlighting Jordan's more-professionalized approach through Centers of Excellence may be preferable.

On the economic dimension, a mix of bilateral and multilateral engagement is a wise approach as it operates as a hedge in a volatile region. Continued bilateral economic engagement, building from the FTAs with Bahrain and Oman, is likely to be the most viable economic approach for the United States vis-à-vis the GCC in the short term. In addition to bolstering U.S. trade with the GCC nations, which will benefit both the United States and these nations, bilateral FTAs should induce economic diversification within the GCC by encouraging export diversification.[10] Analogously, bilateral investment treaties may encourage improved financial practices among the GCC, and create new investment opportunities for the United States, though the effectiveness of bilateral investment treaties in encouraging flows of FDI is not well established.[11]

---

[10]  Previous analyses have found that trade liberalization is associated with increased export diversification (see, for example, Christian Volpe Martincus and Sandra Milena Gomez, "Trade Policy and Export Diversification: What Should Colombia Expect from the FTA with the United States?" *The International Trade Journal*, Vol. 24, No. 2, 2010, pp. 100–148; Alberto Amurgo-Pacheco and Martha Denisse Pierola, "Patterns of Export Diversification in Developing Countries: Intensive and Extensive Margins," *Policy Research Working Paper* 4473, Washington, D.C.: World Bank, 2008).

[11]  For a quantitative analysis of bilateral investment treaties signed during 1980–2004, see Wasseem Mina, "Do Bilateral Investment Treaties Encourage FDI in the GCC Countries?" *African Review of Economics and Finance*, Vol. 2, No. 1, December 2010. For a more general review of bilateral investment treaties effectiveness, see Susan Rose-Ackerman and Jennifer Tobin, "Foreign Direct Investment and the Business Environment in Developing Countries: The Impact of Bilateral Investment Treaties," Yale Law & Economics Research Paper, No. 293, May 2, 2005.

However, the United States should continue to explore the opportunity for multilateral economic agreements, building from the recently agreed upon U.S.–GCC TIFA.[12] Though less likely to occur within our ten-year time frame, multilateral engagement—either in the form of a regional FTA or multilateral investment treaty (MIT)—would benefit both the United States and the GCC. Although the particulars of these agreements may be less advantageous to the United States, as the United States tends to get a "better deal" in bilateral agreements, this would give the United States increased access to all six economies simultaneously. For the GCC, this could support enhanced economic integration, likely for the benefit of all six nations. As an example, an MIT would require the GCC to harmonize financial practices in order to enter into such a treaty,[13] which would enhance the ability of private and public investors to focus resources toward productive enterprises.

Another potential long-term initiative would be to support the development of a GCC regional development organization. Patterned after the post–World War II U.S. economic engagement strategy in Europe,[14] which was successful in enhancing European political and economic integration,[15] this organization would give equal representa-

---

[12] Office of the U.S. Trade Representative, 2012.

[13] An MIT also has the advantage of being a natural next step from the TIFAs, which are usually a precursor to an FTA or MIT.

[14] The economies of the GCC today share many characteristics with the nations of Europe following World War II, namely, the availability of robust investment resources to support productive economic activity (most investment in Europe during this period was from domestic savings), the presence of distortionary domestic economic policies, and a variety of political and economic impediments to regional financial and trade integration (see Barry Eichengreen, "Lessons from the Marshall Plan," *World Development Report 2011*, 2010). Although the GCC lacks the history of regional economic integration and established industrial base from which Europeans benefited, the persistence of (1) the GCC as an institution and an ambition of the region and (2) the rapid growth of the nonoil sectors within the GCC in recent years suggest that each may be addressed.

[15] Fostering economic integration across the nations of Europe was a key goal, and one of the key successes, of U.S. economic policy in the wake of World War II—indeed, "the objectives of the Marshall Plan ... were as much political as economic." Note that the total value of aid provided by the United States under the Marshall Plan was relatively small—around 2.5 percent of the national income of Europe—and the direct economic impacts of this money were limited. However, the political impact of the Marshall Plan was significant.

tion to each of the six GCC nations, though funding would be proportionate to the size of the six economies. Effectively, this organization would entail that all intra–GCC aid be decided laterally, rather than through the bilateral processes that are dominant today.[16] If patterned after the Marshall Plan, this initiative would involve a clear role for the United States as an arbitrator, providing useful cover for GCC leaders to take free market reforms that may entail domestic political costs, because these steps would be taken in the framework of participation in a multinational organization. The GCC states might also use it as a mechanism for coordinating aid to Arab countries outside of the Arab Gulf subregion that are economically underdeveloped and facing strain from hosting a growing refugee burden.

## Limitations on U.S. Influence

In planning engagement with its GCC partners, the United States will need to be cognizant of its limitations in shaping partner behavior. As the primary regional security guarantor and equipper of choice, it may be tempting for the United States to take the lead in shaping the regional security order. But the GCC states, Iraq, Iran, and even non-Gulf powers like Israel and Turkey, will all have some degree of influence over the order that emerges. Moreover, some in the region perceive the United States as a declining power at the same time that Saudi Arabia and the Emirates are showing increased self-confidence and willingness to operate independently of Washington. This suggests the United States should be working toward the goal of shaping the evolution of the regional security order but without the hubris that Washington can design or "own" it.

---

These political impacts were both regional, as intraregional cooperation was encouraged by the creation of a regional body that would determine how all aid would be spent, and domestic, as U.S. conditionality required domestic pro-market reforms. See Eichengreen, 2010.

[16]  Faysal Itani, "The Promise and Perils of Gulf Aid," Atlantic Council, 2013. In this article, Itani argues that "the secrecy of foreign aid and investment decisions makes it difficult for GCC states to coordinate aid efforts, and impossible if their regional interests diverge."

Politically, the United States also faces significant constraints in promoting more-inclusive and participatory governance; not least of which is Washington's own track record in prioritizing stability over reform. The need to reassure partners that are skeptical of U.S. intentions after the Iran nuclear deal leaves the United States with less political capital to push partners on a reform agenda. Arab publics in general, and Arab Gulf publics in particular, are also reticent to embrace transitions in light of regional tumult and growing insecurity. That said, the United States needs consistency in its messaging on human rights; an improved human rights climate in the Arab Gulf would not only align with U.S. values, but would have practical value for the United States and the GCC countries in countering violent extremism. While conditions do not appear ripe for the pursuit of deep political reform, the United States should continue to raise human rights concerns with the GCC states and press for improvements on the basis of values and security benefits.

In the economic dimension, the United States has the advantage of exploring initiatives with the GCC without the same level of baggage that exists in the security and political realms. Economic engagement with the Gulf does not inflame the same sensitivities as security cooperation that often carries domestic political costs for Arab Gulf leaders. And although the U.S. share of the world economy is declining, the United States remains an attractive consumer market, a leader in innovation, and a stabilizing force in an era of global volatility. This suggests that a general shift toward economic initiatives may be a more fertile area for engagement between the United States and its Gulf partners than the political and security dimensions.

# Abbreviations

| | |
|---|---|
| EU | European Union |
| FDI | foreign direct investment |
| FTA | free trade agreement |
| GCC | Gulf Cooperation Council |
| GDP | gross domestic product |
| GIC | Gulf Investment Corporation |
| ISIL | Islamic State in the Levant |
| JCPOA | Joint Comprehensive Plan of Action |
| MB | Muslim Brotherhood |
| MIT | multilateral investment treaty |
| NAFTA | North American Free Trade Agreement |
| NATO | North Atlantic Treaty Organization |
| OPEC | Organization of the Petroleum Exporting Countries |
| PSF | Peninsula Shield Force |
| TIFA | Trade and Investment Framework Agreement |
| UAE | United Arab Emirates |
| UEA | Unified Economic Agreement |
| UK | United Kingdom |

# References

"118,000 Families To Receive Meat Subsidy Payouts," Bahrain News Agency, October 2, 2015.

AidData, "About Our Data Products," web page, undated. As of March 9, 2016: http://aiddata.org/about-our-data-products

Air Transport Action Group, "Aviation Benefits Beyond Borders: Providing Employment, Trade Links, Tourism and Support for Sustainable Development Through Air Travel," March 2012. As of March 24, 2016: http://www.obsa.org/Lists/Documentacion/Attachments/519/Aviation_benefits _beyond_borders_EN.pdf

Ali, Sumaya, *GCC Economics: UAE-Iran's Trade Relations*, Securities and Investment Company, July 30, 2015. As of March 9, 2016: http://www.marketstoday.net/includes/download.php?file=rr_30072015170259. pdf&lang=en&s=3483&m=research

Alpen Capital, "GCC Aviation Industry," March 3, 2014.

Amurgo-Pacheco, Alberto, and Martha Denisse Pierola, "Patterns of Export Diversification in Developing Countries: Intensive and Extensive Margins," *Policy Research Working Paper 4473*, Washington, D.C.: World Bank, 2008.

Anthony, John Duke, "Strategic Dynamics of Iran-GCC Relations," in Jean-Francois Seznec and Mimi Kirk, eds., *Industrialization in the Gulf: A Socioeconomic Revolution*, Washington, D.C.: Routledge, 2010.

Asiya Investments, "Lower Oil Prices May Spur the Gulf to Diversify," Dubai, 2015.

Badawi, Nada, "Qatari Men Report for First Day of Mandatory National Service," *Doha News*, April 1, 2014. As of March 9, 2016: http://dohanews.co/first-day-mandatory-national-service-kicks-2000-recruits/

"Bahrain Postpones Plan To Remove Meat Subsidies," Reuters, September 2, 2015.

Bailey, Rob, "Food Security Issue for GCC is Linked to Supply, Not Prices," *The National*, November 11, 2013. As of March 9, 2016:
http://www.thenational.ae/thenationalconversation/comment/
food-security-issue-for-gcc-is-linked-to-supply-not-prices

Baldwin-Edwards, Martin, "Labour Immigration and Labour Markets in the GCC Countries: National Patterns and Trends," Kuwait Programme on Development, Governance and Globalisation in the Gulf States, London: The London School of Economics and Political Science, No. 15, 2011. As of March 8, 2016:
http://eprints.lse.ac.uk/55239/

Barnett, Michael, and F. Gregory Gause III, "Caravans in Opposite Directions: Society, State, and the Development of Community in the Gulf Cooperation Council," in Emanuel Adler and Michael Barnett, 1st ed., *Security Communities*, Cambridge, UK: Cambridge University Press, 1998, pp. 161–197.

Beblawi, Hazem, "The Rentier State in the Arab World," in Giacomo Luciani, ed., *The Arab State*, Berkeley: University of California Press, 1990.

BMI Research, "Saudi Companies Well Positioned for Regional Expansion," web page, May 29, 2015. As of March 21, 2016:
http://www.bmiresearch.com/news-and-views/
saudi-companies-well-positioned-for-regional-expansion-fooddrink

Braun, Joachim, and Maximo Torrero, *Implementing Physical and Virtual Food Reserves to Protect the Poor and Prevent Market Failure*, policy brief, No. 10, International Food Policy Research Institute, February 2009.

Callen, Tim, Reda Cherif, Fuad Hasanov, Amgad Hegazy, and Padamja Khandelwal, "Economic Diversification in the GCC: Past, Present, and Future," staff discussion notes, No. 14/12, International Monetary Fund, 2014.

Carpenter, Claudia, and Sarmad Khan, "UAE Removes Fuel Subsidy as Oil Drop Hurts Arab Economies," Bloomberg, July 21, 2015. As of March 9, 2016:
http://www.bloomberg.com/news/
articles/2015-07-22/u-a-e-to-link-gasoline-price-to-global-markets-effect-aug-1

Cochrane, Paul, "GCC Starts Tightening its Belt on Glimmers of Future Austerity," *Middle East Eye*, April 21, 2015. As of March 9, 2016:
http://www.middleeasteye.net/columns/
gcc-starts-tightening-its-belt-glimmers-future-austerity-gcc-1500-529206777

The Cooperation Council for the Arab States of the Gulf, homepage, undated(a). As of August 5, 2015:
https://www.gcc-sg.org/index-2.html

———, "The Charter," web page, undated(b). As of March 7, 2016:
https://www.gcc-sg.org/eng/indexfc7a.html

————, "GCC Joint Defense Agreement," web page, December 2000. As of April 19, 2016:
https://www.gcc-sg.org/eng/index8409.html?action=Sec-Show&ID=49

The Cooperation Council for the Arab States of the Gulf Secretariat General, "The Revised Long-Term Comprehensive Development Strategy for the GCC States: 2010-2025," 2011.

Cordesman, Anthony, *The Gulf Military Balance: Volume I: The Conventional and Asymmetric Dimensions*, Center for Strategic & International Studies, January 2014.

Al-Dasuqi, Ayman Ibrahim, "Muʿadalat al-Istiqrār fī al-Nizhām al-Iqlīmī al-Khalījī" ["The Stability Dilemma in the Gulf Regional Order"], *Al-Mustaqbal al-ʿArabi Journal*, No. 434, April 2015.

Davis, Lynn E., Jeffrey Martini, Alireza Nader, Dalia Dassa Kaye, James T. Quinlivan, and Paul S. Steinberg, *Iran's Nuclear Future: Critical U.S. Policy Choices*, Santa Monica, Calif.: RAND Corporation, MG-1087-AF, 2011. As of February 25, 2016:
http://www.rand.org/pubs/monographs/MG1087.html

Doing Business Group, "Doing Business 2010: Reforming Through Difficult Times," World Bank, Global Indicators Group, September 9, 2009. As of March 8, 2016:
http://www.doingbusiness.org/reports/global-reports/doing-business-2010

————, "Doing Business 2016: Measuring Regulatory Quality and Efficiency," World Bank, Global Indicators Group, October 27, 2015. As of March 8, 2016:
http://www.doingbusiness.org/reports/global-reports/doing-business-2016

"Duwāl al-Khalīj Tadaʿū al-ʿIraq ila Waqf Tadakhulātihi bi Shuʾūn al-Bahrain" ["The Gulf Countries Call on Iraq to Cease its Interventions in the Affairs of Bahrain"], *Al-Arabi al-Jadid*, June 22, 2015.

The Economist Intelligence Unit, "GCC Customs Union Up and Running," *The Economist,* January 13, 2015.

Eichengreen, Barry, "Lessons from the Marshall Plan," *World Development Report 2011*, 2010.

Emirates 24/7 Business, "Qatar Airways Boss Slams U.S. Airlines on Subsidy Allegations," web page, July 10, 2015. As of March 8, 2016:
http://www.emirates247.com/business/corporate/qatar-airways-boss-slams-us-airlines-on-subsidy-allegations-2015-05-08-1.589997

Frost & Sullivan, *Strategic Insight on the GCC Rail Sector*, October 21, 2011.

Freedom House, "About Freedom in the World: An Annual Study of Political Rights and Civil Liberties," web page, undated. As of March 7, 2016:
https://freedomhouse.org/report-types/freedom-world

Fulton, Will, and Ariel Farrar-Wellman, "GCC-Iran Foreign Relations," Iran Tracker, July 21, 2011. As of March 9, 2016: http://www.irantracker.org/foreign-relations/gcc-iran-foreign-relations

Gause, F. Gregory III, "Threats and Threat Perception in the Persian Gulf Region," *Middle East Policy*, Vol. 14, No. 2, Summer 2007.

———, *The International Relations of the Persian Gulf*, Cambridge, UK: Cambridge University Press, 2009.

GCC Statistical Center, "Statistics," web page, undated. As of March 9, 2016: http://gccstat.org/en/

"GCC Studies Jordan, Morocco Membership Bids," *Gulf News*, May 11, 2011. As of March 7, 2016: http://gulfnews.com/news/gulf/saudi-arabia/ gcc-studies-jordan-morocco-membership-bids-1.806159

Gengler, Justin, "Royal Factionalism, the Khawalid, and the Securitization of 'the Shi'a Problem' in Bahrain," *Journal of Arabian Studies: Arabia, the Gulf, and the Red Sea*, Vol. 1, No. 3, 2013.

GIC—*See* Gulf Investment Corporation.

Goldberg, Jeffrey, "The Atlantic's Jeffrey Goldberg Interviews President Obama," *The Atlantic*, May 21, 2015.

Gulf Investment Corporation, "GIC Financial Results 2014," web page, undated(a). As of March 8, 2016: https://www.gic.com.kw/en/about-us/financial-results2012/

———, "Our History," web page, undated(b). As of March 8, 2016: https://www.gic.com.kw/en/about-us/history/

Guzansky, Yoel, "Defense Cooperation in the Arabian Gulf: The Peninsula Shield Force Put to the Test," *Middle Eastern Studies*, Vol. 50, No. 4, May 2014.

———, "The Foreign Policy Tools of Small Powers: Strategic Hedging in the Persian Gulf," *Middle East Policy*, Vol. XXII, No. 1, 2015a.

———, "Strategic Hedging by Non-Great Powers," in Aharon Klieman, ed., *Great Powers and Geopolitics: International Affairs in a Rebalancing World*, Springer, 2015b.

Al-Habas, Khalid bin Nayef, "al-Sa'udīya wa Mas'ūlīyat al-Qīyāda al-Iqlīmīya" ["Saudi Arabia and the Responsibility of Regional Leadership"], *al-Hayat*, May 13, 2015.

Habibi, Nader, "The Impact of Sanctions on Iran-GCC Economic Relations," Middle East Brief, No. 45, Brandeis University Crown Center for Middle East Studies, November 2010. As of March 9, 2016: http://www.brandeis.edu/crown/publications/meb/MEB45.pdf

Habibi, Nader, and Eckart Woertz, "U.S.–Arab Economic Relations and the Obama Administration," Middle East Brief, No. 34, Brandeis University Crown Center for Middle East Studies, February 2009. As of March 9, 2016: http://www.brandeis.edu/crown/publications/meb/MEB34.pdf

Hagel, Chuck, speech delivered at Manama Dialogue, Manama, Bahrain, December 7, 2013. As of March 9, 2016: http://archive.defense.gov/speeches/speech.aspx?speechid=1824

Haldane, John, "GCC: Moving Towards Unity," *Washington Report on Middle East Affairs*, February 4, 1985. As of March 8, 2016: http://www.wrmea.org/1985-february-4/gcc-moving-towards-unity.html

Hertog, Steffen, "The Private Sector and Reform in the Gulf Cooperation Council," research paper, Kuwait Programme on Development, Governance, and Globalisation in the Gulf States, London School of Economics, July 2013. As of March 21, 2016: http://www.lse.ac.uk/middleEastCentre/kuwait/documents/the-private-sector-and-reform-in-the-gcc.pdf

———, *GCC Economic Integration: Focus on Nitty-Gritty of Convergence Rather Than High Profile Projects*, Gulf Research Center, September 2014.

Ibish, Hussein, *For Gulf Countries, Iran's Regional Behavior Overshadows Nuclear Deal*, The Arab Gulf States Institute in Washington, July 7, 2015. As of March 9, 2016: http://www.agsiw.org/for-gulf-countries-irans-regional-behavior-overshadows-nuclear-deal/

Institute of International Finance, *GCC: Strong Diversified Growth, Limited Risks*, Washington, D.C., May 2014

International Monetary Fund, "Direction of Trade Statistics (DOTS)," web page, February 24, 2016. As of March 9, 2016: http://data.imf.org/?sk=9D6028D4-F14A-464C-A2F2-59B2CD424B85

Isma'il, Rashed Ahmed Rashed, "Sīyāsāt Buldān Majlis al-Taʿāwun al-Khalījī tijāh Tadāʿīyāt Azmat Rabīʿ al-Thawrāt al-ʿArabīya (Bahrain Anmūdhjan)" ["The Policies of the Gulf Cooperation Council Towards the Crisis of the Arab Spring Revolutions (Bahrain as an Example)"], *The Arab Journal of Political Science*, Nos. 43 and 44, Summer and Fall 2014.

Itani, Faysal, "The Promise and Perils of Gulf Aid," Atlantic Council, 2013. As of March 9, 2016: http://www.atlanticcouncil.org/blogs/menasource/the-promise-and-perils-of-gulf-aid

Jaffe, Alexandra, "Saudi Ambassador to U.S. Won't Rule Out Building Nukes," CNN, March 27, 2015.

Jain, Shweta, "Power Grid Brings GCC Economies Closer," *Gulf News*, April 25, 2011. As of March 9, 2016:
http://gulfnews.com/business/sectors/features/power-grid-brings-gcc-economies-closer-1.798660

John, Issac, "GCC Expenditure on Track for $172 Billion Projects in 2015," *Khaleej Times*, June 1, 2015. As of March 9, 2016:
http://www.khaleejtimes.com/article/20150601/ARTICLE/306019880/1037

Kahl, Colin H., Melissa G. Dalton, and Matthew Irvine, *Atomic Kingdom: If Iran Builds the Bomb, Will Saudi Arabia Be Next?* Center for a New American Security, February 2013. As of March 9, 2016:
http://www.cnas.org/files/documents/publications/CNAS_AtomicKingdom_Kahl.pdf

Katzman, Kenneth, "Iran, Gulf Security, and U.S. Policy," *Congressional Research Service*, May 28, 2015.

Kaye, Dalia Dassa, and Jeffrey Martini, *The Days After a Deal with Iran: Regional Responses to a Final Nuclear Agreement*, Santa Monica, Calif.: RAND Corporation, PE-122-RC, 2014. As of March 9, 2016:
http://www.rand.org/pubs/perspectives/PE122.html

Kaye, Dalia Dassa, and Frederic Wehrey, "A Nuclear Iran: The Reactions of Neighbours," *Survival*, 2007.

Keohane, Robert, "Cooperation and International Regimes," in *Perspectives on World Politics*, Little and Smith, eds., Routledge, 2006.

Kerr, Simeon and Pilita Clark, "UAE Drops Fuel Subsidies to Boost Finances and Cut Emissions," *Financial Times*, July 22, 2015.

"Khitāb Musarrib li Wazīr al-Naft al-Kuwaitī qad Yufāqim al-Azma al-Naftīya ma' al-Sa'udīya" ["A Leaked Message from the Kuwait Oil Minister Could Exacerbate the Oil Crisis with Saudi Arabia"], *Al-Khaleej al-Jadid*, July 29, 2015.

Kinninmont, Jane, *Future Trends in the Gulf*, Chatham House, The Royal Institute of International Affairs, February 19, 2015.

Körner, Kevin, and Oliver Masetti, *GCC in Times of Cheap Oil: An Opportunity for Economic Reform and Diversification*, Deutsche Bank Research, June 2015.

Lawler, Alex, "Saudi-Iran Rivalry Sets Scene for OPEC Showdown Over Output," Reuters, December 6, 2015.

Legrenzi, Matteo, "Did the GCC Make a Difference? Institutional Realities and (Un)Intended Consequences," in Cilja Harders and Matteo Legrenzi, eds., *Beyond Regionalism?: Regional Cooperation, Regionalism and Regionalization in the Middle East*, London: Routledge, 2013.

"Al-Mamlaka, wa al-Imārāt wa al-Bahrain Tashab Sufarā'iha min Qatar" ["The Kingdom, the Emirates and Bahrain Withdraw their Ambassadors from Qatar"], *Al-Riyadh*, March 5, 2014.

Martincus, Christian Volpe, and Sandra Milena Gomez, "Trade Policy and Export Diversification: What Should Colombia Expect from the FTA with the United States?" *The International Trade Journal*, Vol. 24, No. 2, 2010.

Mason, Robert, "The Omani Pursuit of a Large Peninsula Shield Force: A Case Study of a Small State's Search for Security," *British Journal of Middle Eastern Studies*, Vol. 41, No. 4, 2014.

Mina, Wasseem, "Do Bilateral Investment Treaties Encourage FDI in the GCC Countries?" *African Review of Economics and Finance*, Vol. 2, No. 1, December 2010.

Mueller, H.G., "GCC Industrial Development," in G. Luciani, ed., *Resources Blessed: Diversification and the Gulf Development Model*, Berlin: Gerlach Press, 2012.

Mustafa, Awad, "Hagel: U.S. to Sell Weapons to GCC States as a Block," Defense News, December 7, 2013.

Nechi, Salem, "Assessing Economic and Financial Cooperation and Integration Among the GCC Countries," *Journal of Business & Policy Research*, Vol. 5, No. 1, July 2010.

Obaid, Nawaf, "Actually, Saudi Arabia Could Get a Nuclear Weapon," CNN, June 19, 2015.

Office of the U.S. Trade Representative, "Framework Agreement for Trade, Economic, Investment and Technical Cooperation Between the Cooperation Council for the Arab States and the Government of the United States of America," 2012. As of March 9, 2016:
https://ustr.gov/sites/default/files/uploads/agreements/Trade%20Investment/U.S.-GCC%20TIFA%20Final%20Text%20--%20English%209-25-12.pdf

O'Reilly, Marc J., "Omanibalancing: Oman Confronts an Uncertain Future," *Middle East Journal*, Vol. 52, No. 1, Winter 1998.

Partrick, Neil, "The GCC: Gulf State Integration or Leadership Cooperation?" research paper, Kuwait Programme on Development, Governance, and Globalisation in the Gulf States, London School of Economics, November 2011.

"Private Sector Innovation To Drive GCC Projects," *Arab News*, 2014. As of March 9, 2016:
http://www.arabnews.com/news/economy/613961

"Qatar Ranks Third in Employment of GCC Nationals," *BQ Magazine*, December 9, 2014. As of March 8, 2016:
http://www.bq-magazine.com/economy/2014/12/qatar-ranks-third-employmernt-gcc-nationals

"Qimat ar-Riyādh Tunhī al-Khilāf al-Khalījī maʿ Qatar" ["The Riyadh Summit Ends the Gulf Dispute with Qatar"], *Al-Arabiya*, November 16, 2014.

Rabian, Abdullah bin, "Al-Mamlaka Akbar min al-Riyadh wa al Jidda Ya Sama!" ["Oh Saudi Arabian Monetary Agency: The Kingdom is Bigger than Riyadh and Jidda!"], *al-Hayat*, September 18, 2015.

Razoux, Pierre, "The New Club of Arab Monarchies," *The New York Times*, June 1, 2011.

Rose-Ackerman, Susan, and Jennifer Tobin, "Foreign Direct Investment and the Business Environment in Developing Countries: The Impact of Bilateral Investment Treaties," Yale Law & Economics Research Paper, No. 293, May 2, 2005.

Al-Rumayhi, Muhamad, *Al-Khalīj 2025 [The Gulf 2025]*, Beirut, Lebanon: Dar al-Saqi, 2009.

Salama, Muʿatz, ed., "Ittihād Duwwal al-Khalīj al-ʿArabīya: Afāq al-Mustaqbal" ["The Union of Arab Gulf Countries: Future Horizons"], *Al-Siyāsa Al-Dawlīya Journal*, April 2014.

Salem, Paul, "Kuwait: Politics in a Participatory Emirate," Carnegie Papers, No. 3, Carnegie Endowment for International Peace, June 2007. As of March 8, 2016: http://carnegieendowment.org/files/cmec3_salem_kuwait_final1.pdf

Shediac, Richard, Parag Khanna, Taufiq Rahim, and Hatem A. Samman, *Integrating, Not Integrated: A Scorecard of GCC Economic Integration*, Booz & Company Ideation Center, 2011. As of March 21, 2016: http://static1.squarespace.com/static/565d7420e4b0987eb9f25078/5672d9518169 24fc226b0b66/5672d953816924fc226b0c68/1450367315938/BoozCo-Scorecard-GCC-Economic-Integration.pdf?format=original

Sophia, Mary, "Sun & Sand Sports to Create 500 Jobs Across GCC in 2015," *Gulf Business*, February 2, 2015. As of March 8, 2016: http://gulfbusiness.com/2015/02/sun-sand-sports-create-500-jobs-across-gcc-2015/#.VdPweEJViko

Steinberg, Guido, "Islamism in the Gulf," in Ana Echagüe, ed., *The Gulf States and the Arab Uprisings*, Madrid: FRIDE and the Gulf Research Center, 2013.

Szubin, Andrew, "Beyond The Vote: Implications for the Sanctions Regime on Iran," address to the Washington Institute, September 16, 2015.

Trofimov, Yaroslav, "Saudis Warm to Muslim Brotherhood, Seeking Sunni Unity on Yemen," *The Wall Street Journal*, April 2, 2015.

"UAE Introduces Compulsory Military Service," Al Jazeera, June 8, 2014. As of March 9, 2016: http://www.aljazeera.com/news/middleeast/2014/06/united-arab-emirates-issues-conscription-law-20146872230517860.html

Ulrichsen, Kristian, "Gulf Security: Changing Internal and External Dynamics," London School of Economics, May 2009.

———, "Domestic Implications of the Arab Uprisings in the Gulf," in Ana Echagüe, ed., *The Gulf States and the Arab Uprisings*, Madrid: FRIDE and the Gulf Research Center, 2013.

"Uman Tarfud al-Itthād al-Khalījī wa Tulawwih bi al-Insihāb" ["Oman Rejects the Gulf Union and Intimates Withdrawing"], *Al-Bayan*, December 8, 2013.

UNCTAD—*See* United Nations Conference on Trade and Development.

United Nations Conference on Trade and Development Trade and Development Board: Investment, Enterprise and Development Commission, "Regional Integration and Foreign Direct Investment in Developing and Transition Economies, United Nations, December 3, 2012.

U.S. Department of Defense, "Eagle Resolve Exercise Draws Worldwide Participation," March 20, 2015. As of March 9, 2016: http://www.defense.gov/news/newsarticle.aspx?id=128420

Vardhan, Julie, "Internationalization and the Changing Paradigm of Higher Education in the GCC Countries, *Sage Open*, Vol. 5, No. 2, April 2015.

Walt, Stephen M., "Why Alliances Endure or Collapse," *Survival: Global Politics and Strategy*, Vol. 39, No. 1, 1997.

Wehrey, Frederic, Theodore W. Karasik, Alireza Nader, Jeremy J. Ghez, Lydia Hansell, and Robert A. Guffey, *Saudi-Iranian Relations Since the Fall of Saddam: Rivalry, Cooperation, and Implications for U.S. Policy*, Santa Monica, Calif.: RAND Corporation, MG-840-SRF, 2009. As of April 12, 2016: http://www.rand.org/pubs/monographs/MG840.html

The White House, "U.S.–Gulf Cooperation Council Camp David Joint Statement," Washington, D.C., May 14, 2015. As of March 9, 2016: https://www.whitehouse.gov/the-press-office/2015/05/14/us-gulf-cooperation-council-camp-david-joint-statement

———, "Readout of the President's Meeting with Saudi Foreign Minister Adel Al-Jubeir," press release, July 17, 2015. As of March 9, 2016: https://www.whitehouse.gov/the-press-office/2015/07/17/readout-president%E2%80%99s-meeting-saudi-foreign-minister-adel-al-jubeir

Woertz, Eckart, *Financial Aspects of GCC Unification Efforts*, Gulf Research Center, August 2014.

World Bank, "Economic Integration in the Gulf Cooperation Council (GCC)," 2010.

———, "Iran: Lifting of Sanctions Will Lower Oil Prices and Boost Domestic Economy if Managed Well," press release, Washington, D.C., August 10, 2015. As of March 9, 2016:
http://www.worldbank.org/en/news/press-release/2015/08/10/iran-lifting-sanctions-will-lower-oil-prices-and-boost-domestic-economy-if-managed-well

World Intellectual Property Organization, "The Unified Economic Agreement Between the Countries of the Gulf Cooperation Council," undated. As of March 7, 2016:
http://www.wipo.int/edocs/lexdocs/treaties/en/gcc/trt_gcc.pdf

Young, Karen, *Imagining Economic Opportunity in Iran*, The Arab Gulf States Institute in Washington, July 16, 2015. As of March 9, 2016:
http://www.agsiw.org/imagining-economic-opportunity-in-iran/

Zorob, Anja, "Oman Caught Between the GCC Customs Union and Bilateral Trade with the U.S.," in Steffen Wippel, eds., *Regionalizing Oman: Political, Economic and Social Dynamics*, June 2013.